I SPY
Games to Learn Alphabet

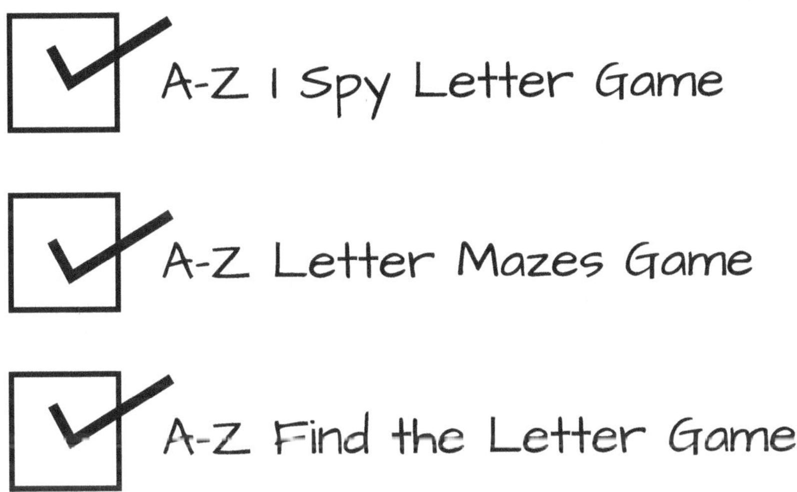

- ☑ A-Z I Spy Letter Game
- ☑ A-Z Letter Mazes Game
- ☑ A-Z Find the Letter Game

This book belongs to

_ _

1) Conversation

Have a conversation with your child about the activity book that you can do with your children.

2) What did you learn

This book contains 26 alphabet picture tracing worksheets for learning the alphabet letter from A to Z.

The first page is the i spy game, children will build visual discrimination skills as they search for the correct letter amongst letters with similar characteristics

The second page is the letter mazes these engaging mazes allow children to follow the path of uppercase and lowercase letters from start to finish.

The third page is the find the letter contains for each of the uppercase and lowercase letters of the alphabet, Children will need to search for the correct letter and coloring it in.

3) Goal

When each activity is complete Check it off in the box provided when they do the activity.

Games to Learn Alphabet
can you do them all?

- [ ] 1. Letter A - a
- [ ] 2. Letter B - b
- [ ] 3. Letter C - c
- [ ] 4. Letter D - d
- [ ] 5. Letter E - e
- [ ] 6. Letter F - f
- [ ] 7. Letter G - g
- [ ] 8. Letter H - h
- [ ] 9. Letter I - i
- [ ] 10. Letter J - j
- [ ] 11. Letter K - k
- [ ] 12. Letter L - l
- [ ] 13. Letter M - m
- [ ] 14. Letter N - n
- [ ] 15. Letter O - o
- [ ] 16. Letter P - p
- [ ] 17. Letter Q - q
- [ ] 18. Letter R - r
- [ ] 19. Letter S - s
- [ ] 20. Letter T - t
- [ ] 21. Letter U - u
- [ ] 22. Letter V - v
- [ ] 23. Letter W - w
- [ ] 24. Letter X - x
- [ ] 25. Letter Y - y
- [ ] 26. Letter Z - z

I Spy Letter

Highlight the uppercase and
lowercase that start with the letter you are learning.

Aa Aa Aa Aa

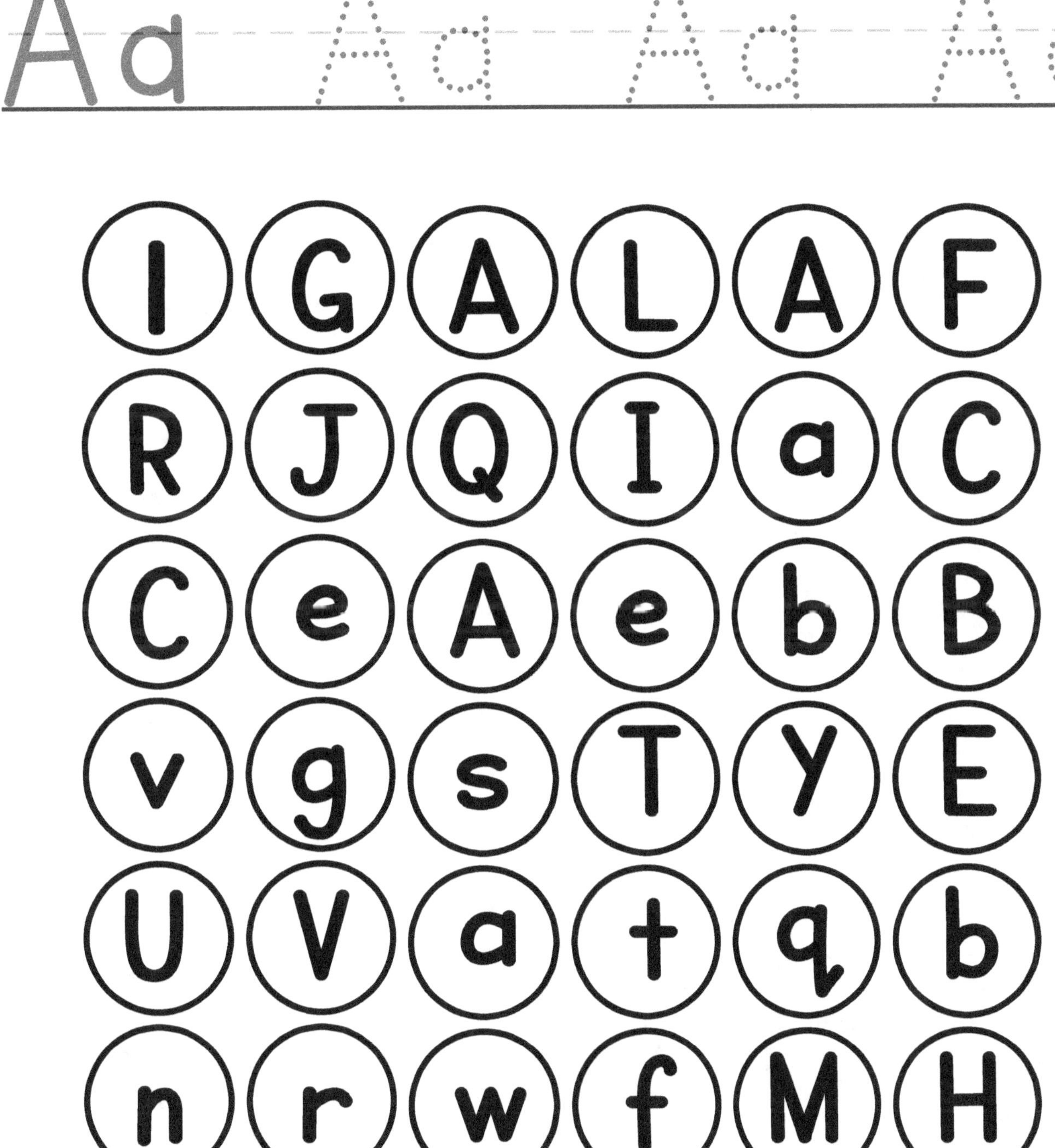

Letter Mazes

Highlight the uppercase and
lowercase that start with the letter you are learning.

A a   A a   A a   A a

A	a	A	G	e	o	I	K
B	n	a	R	q	l	G	g
S	B	a	A	a	t	R	s
t	m	l	k	A	w	E	r
b	l	A	a	A	B	N	c
g	Z	a	g	T	o	S	e
w	o	A	k	A	a	a	9
l	b	A	A	a	Q	A	a

Find the Letter

Highlight the uppercase and
lowercase that start with the letter you are learning.

Aa Aa Aa Aa

A F a G

O T A

a

J W E K

Y

A C D

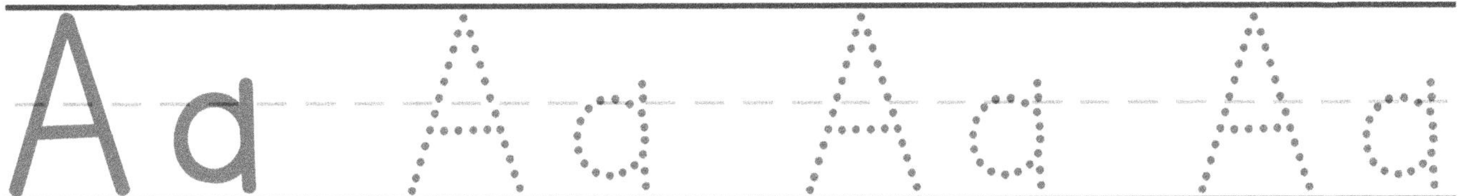

I Spy Letter

Highlight the uppercase and
lowercase that start with the letter you are learning.

B b   B b   B b   B b

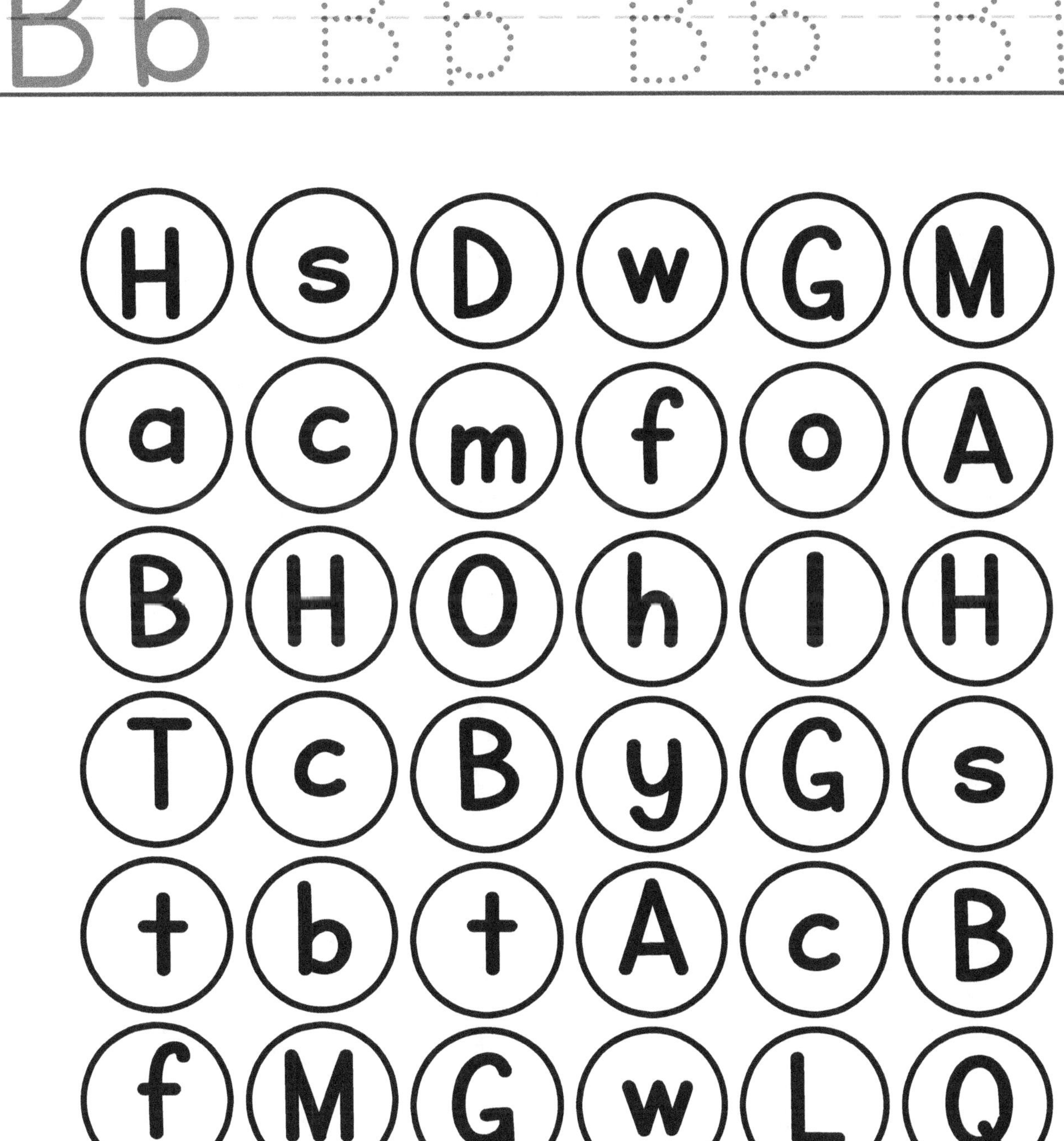

Letter Mazes

Highlight the uppercase and
lowercase that start with the letter you are learning.

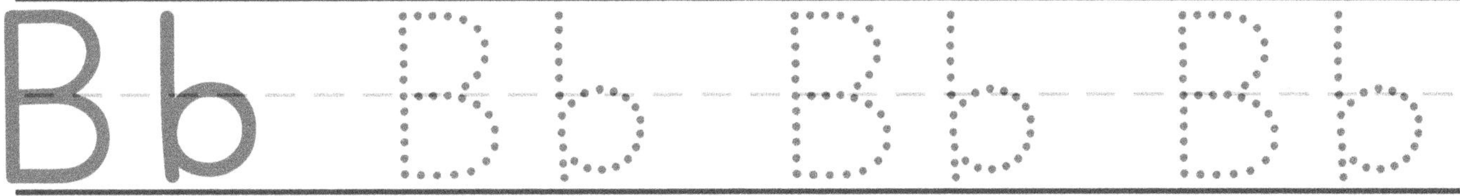

Bb Bb Bb Bb

b	B	X	Z	a	F	D	S
t	b	B	B	b	b	B	I
n	B	D	B	b	t	b	O
b	b	l	B	7	w	B	b
b	l	i	b	D	B	N	b
b	Z	a	B	T	B	b	B
B	B	b	b	b	B	S	K
w	o	p	p	S	b	B	b

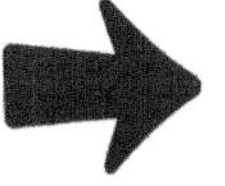

Find the Letter

Highlight the uppercase and
lowercase that start with the letter you are learning.

Bb Bb Bb Bb

S B T U
X L B
O
P b C I
Z b
B A

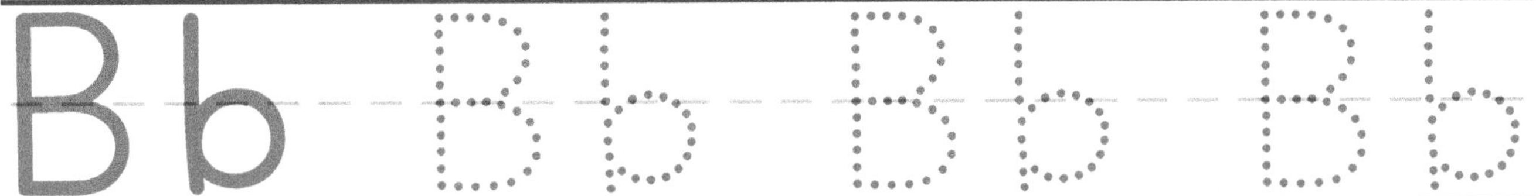

I Spy Letter

Highlight the uppercase and
lowercase that start with the letter you are learning.

C c   C c   C c   C c

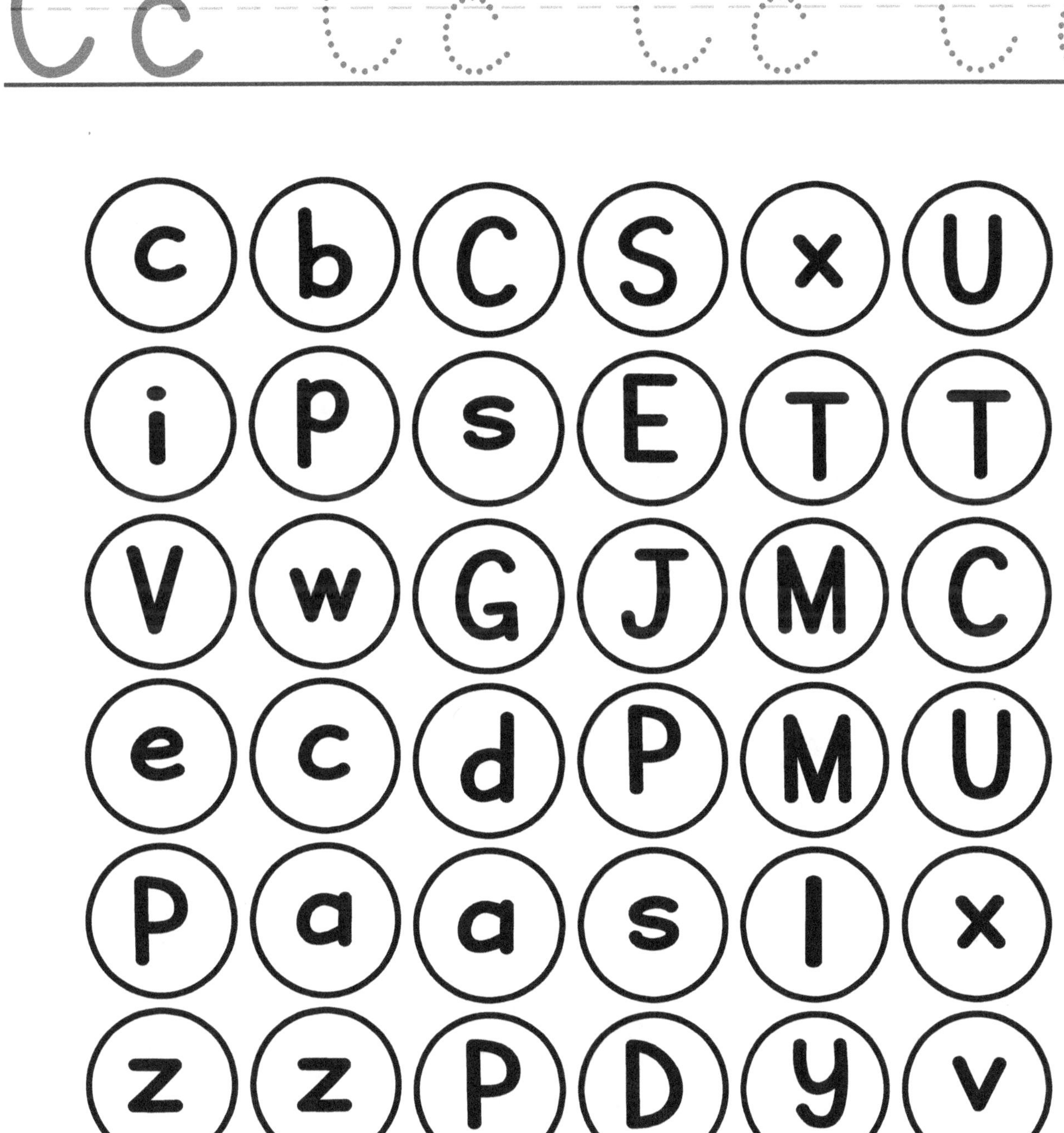

Letter Mazes

Highlight the uppercase and
lowercase that start with the letter you are learning.

Cc Cc Cc Cc

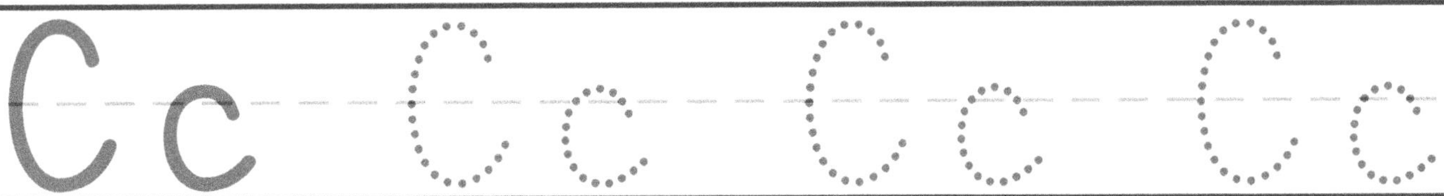

c	c	C	C	T	o	S	e
E	a	A	c	c	C	c	W
w	g	4	G	b	t	C	s
c	c	C	k	C	c	c	r
C	l	C	l	C	G	N	T
C	Z	c	c	C	o	S	S
c	p	E	n	r	h	S	G
C	C	C	C	c	C	c	c

Find the Letter

Highlight the uppercase and
lowercase that start with the letter you are learning.

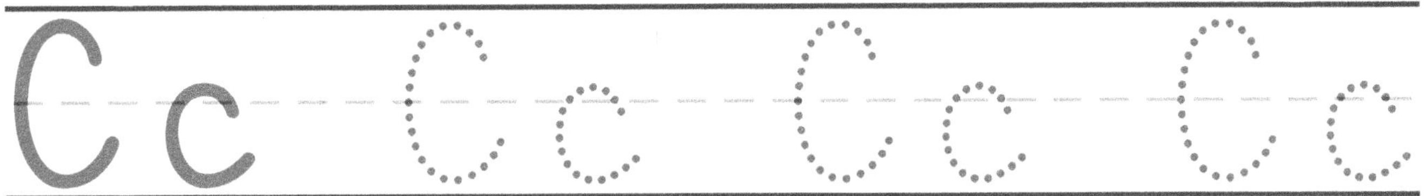

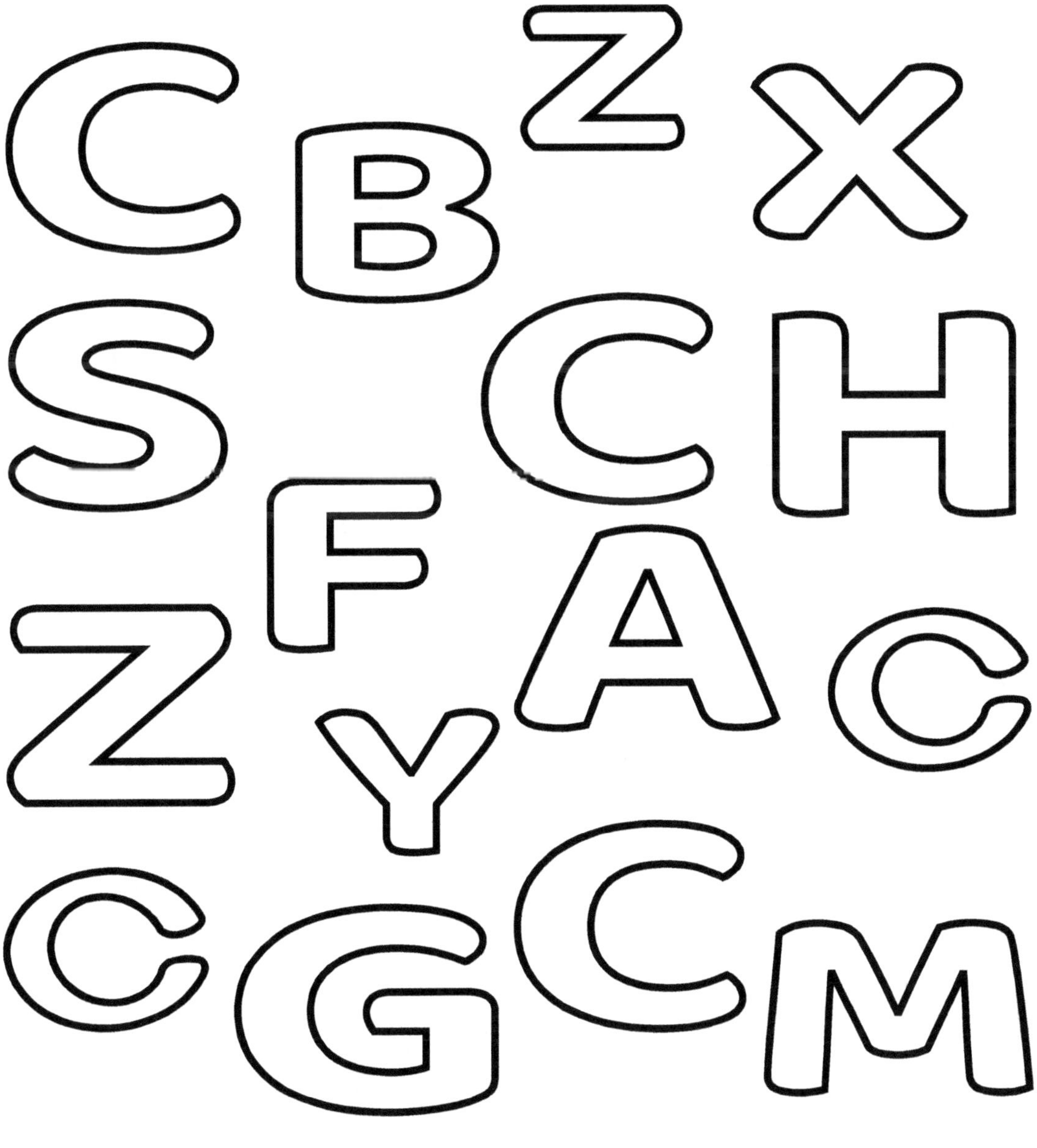

I Spy Letter

Highlight the uppercase and
lowercase that start with the letter you are learning.

Dd Dd Dd Dd

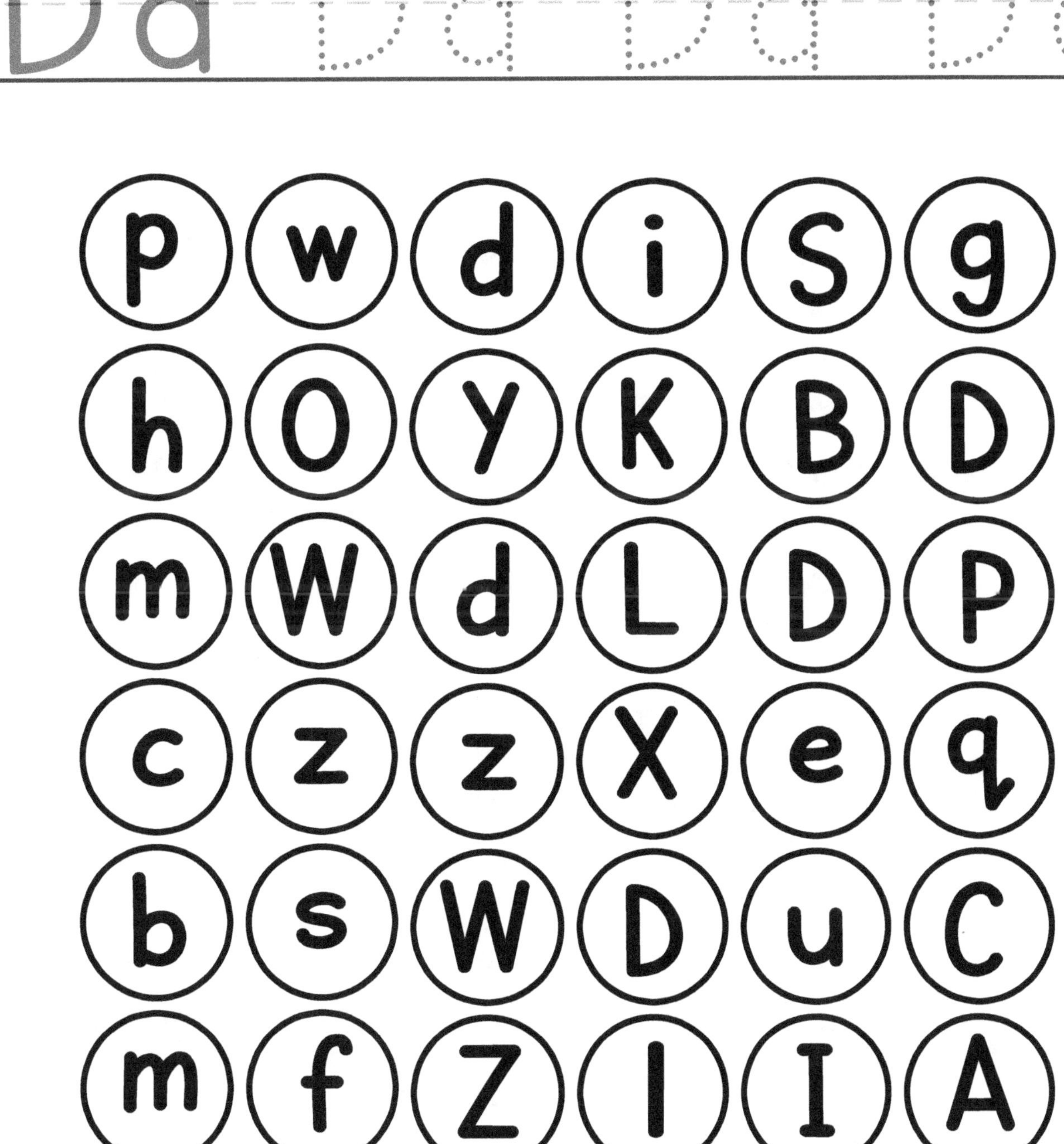

Letter Mazes

Highlight the uppercase and
lowercase that start with the letter you are learning.

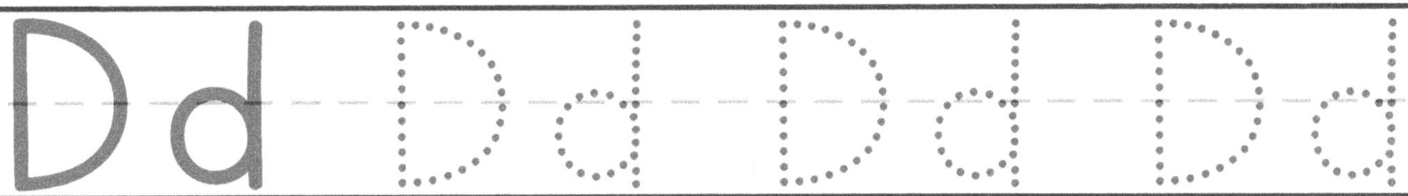

d	D	D	b	a	F	D	S
q	b	d	q	q	p	q	b
d	d	d	p	D	d	D	s
d	s	k	k	D	p	D	b
D	b	i	l	d	n	d	c
D	d	d	B	d	r	d	T
V	o	D	W	d	T	D	W
P	w	D	D	d	8	D	d

Find the Letter

Highlight the uppercase and
lowercase that start with the letter you are learning.

I Spy Letter

Highlight the uppercase and
lowercase that start with the letter you are learning.

E e   E e   E e   E e

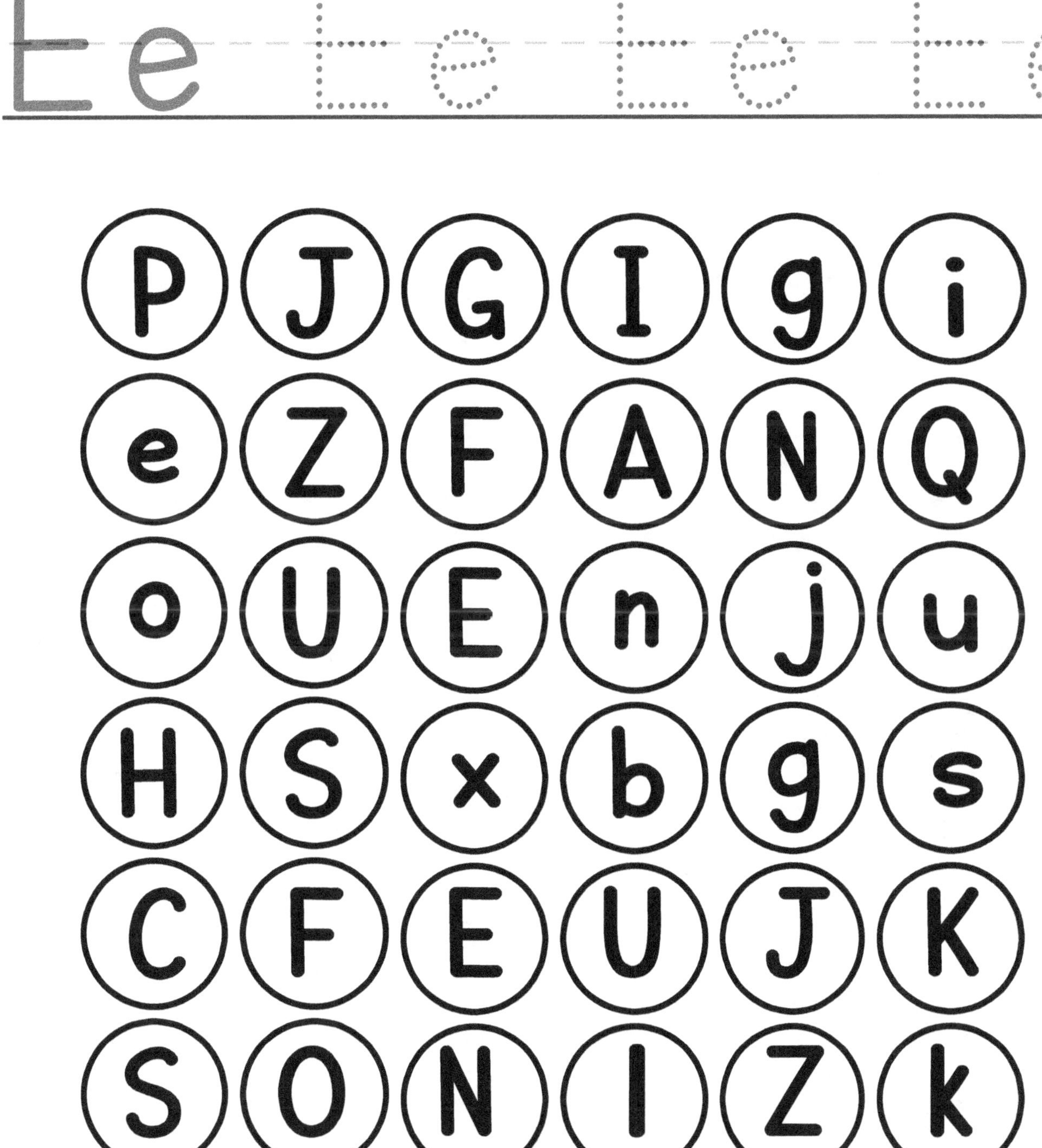

Letter Mazes

Highlight the uppercase and
lowercase that start with the letter you are learning.

Ee   Ee   Ee   Ee

E	e	e	E	t	e	e	E
s	n	B	e	t	E	Y	e
h	B	E	E	y	e	y	e
2	m	E	k	B	e	g	E
E	l	E	e	e	E	n	E
T	Z	a	B	T	o	r	E
W	o	E	W	V	N	S	e
O	Q	d	S	H	r	V	e

Find the Letter

Highlight the uppercase and
lowercase that start with the letter you are learning.

I Spy Letter

Highlight the uppercase and
lowercase that start with the letter you are learning.

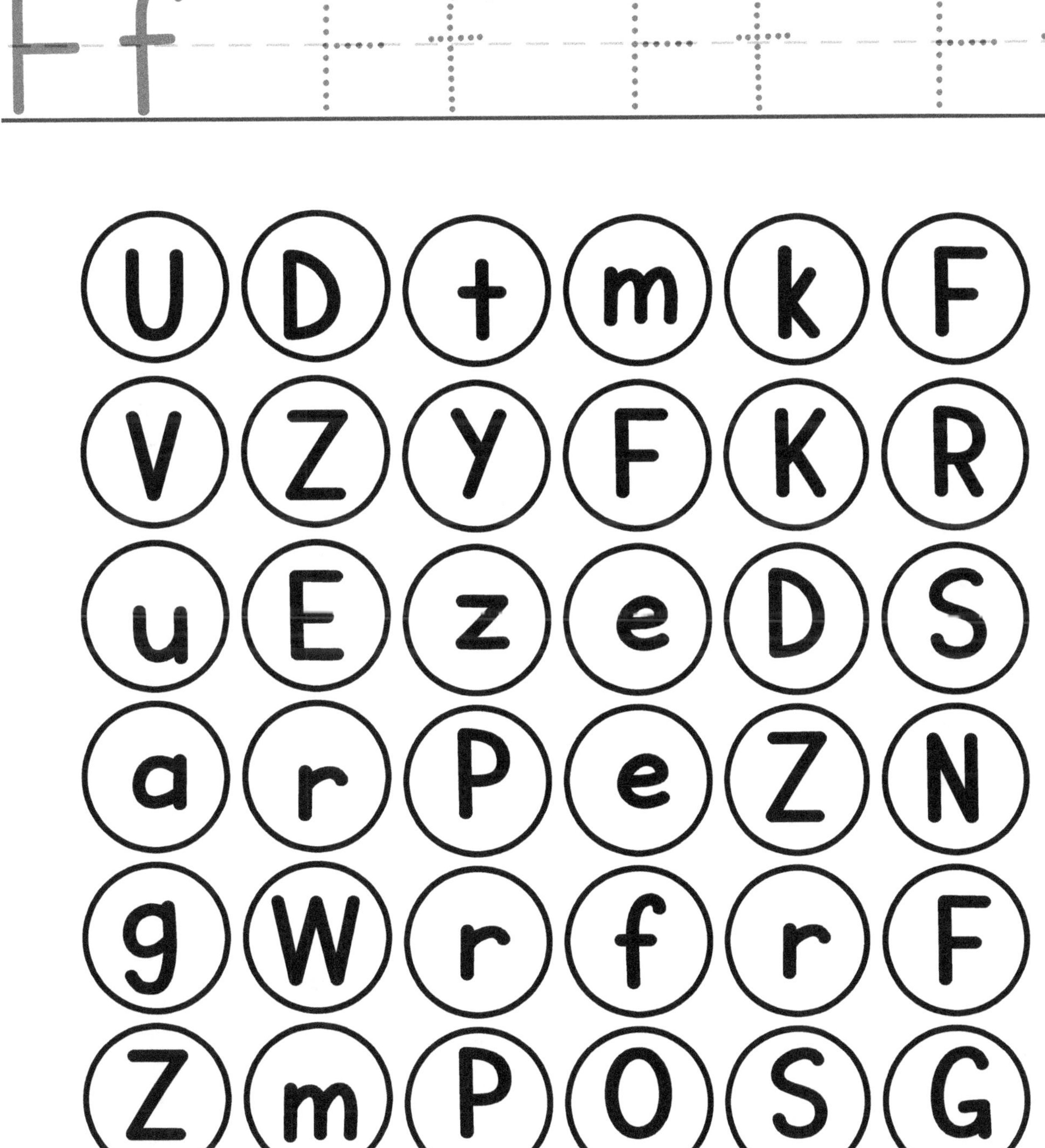

Letter Mazes

Highlight the uppercase and
lowercase that start with the letter you are learning.

F f   F f   F f   F f

f	F	f	F	f	H	i	y
l	t	b	s	f	l	e	S
b	B	D	d	f	B	e	M
F	f	F	F	F	r	E	O
f	l	i	l	m	B	N	N
f	Z	f	f	F	f	F	S
F	5	F	W	V	N	F	e
f	f	F	F	y	r	N	f	f

Find the Letter

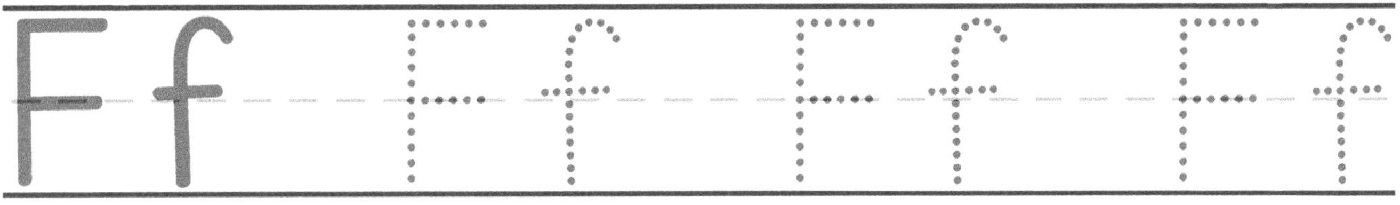

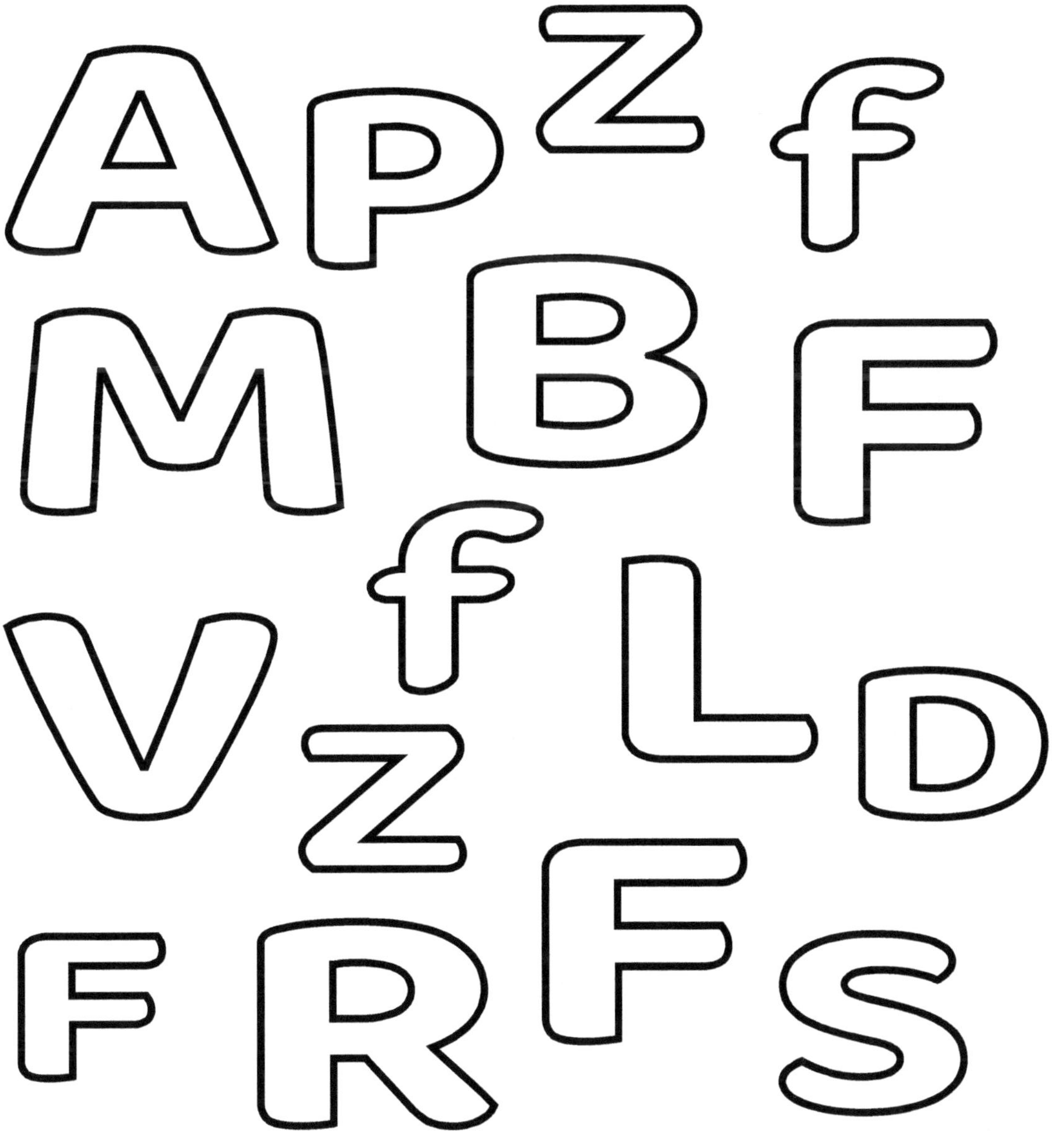

I Spy Letter

Highlight the uppercase and
lowercase that start with the letter you are learning.

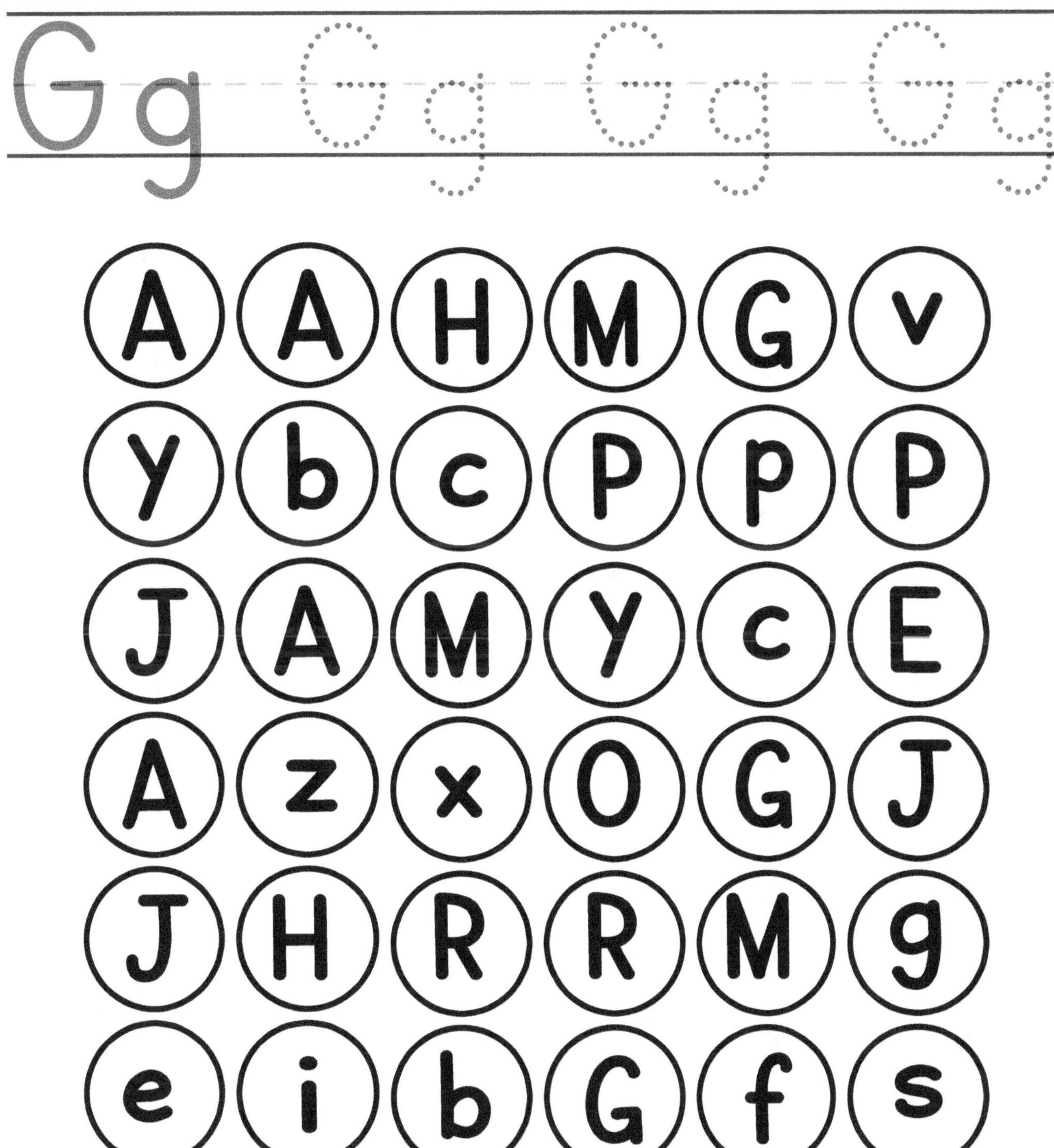

Letter Mazes

Highlight the uppercase and
lowercase that start with the letter you are learning.

G g   G g   G g   G g

G	g	U	G	G	g	g	g
r	g	o	g	q	l	k	g
p	G	W	g	b	t	g	G
3	G	g	g	Q	w	d	g
e	E	e	l	m	G	g	G
F	Z	C	g	G	G	S	f
V	o	e	g	r	N	S	R
e	E	Y	g	G	g	g	G

Find the Letter

Highlight the uppercase and
lowercase that start with the letter you are learning.

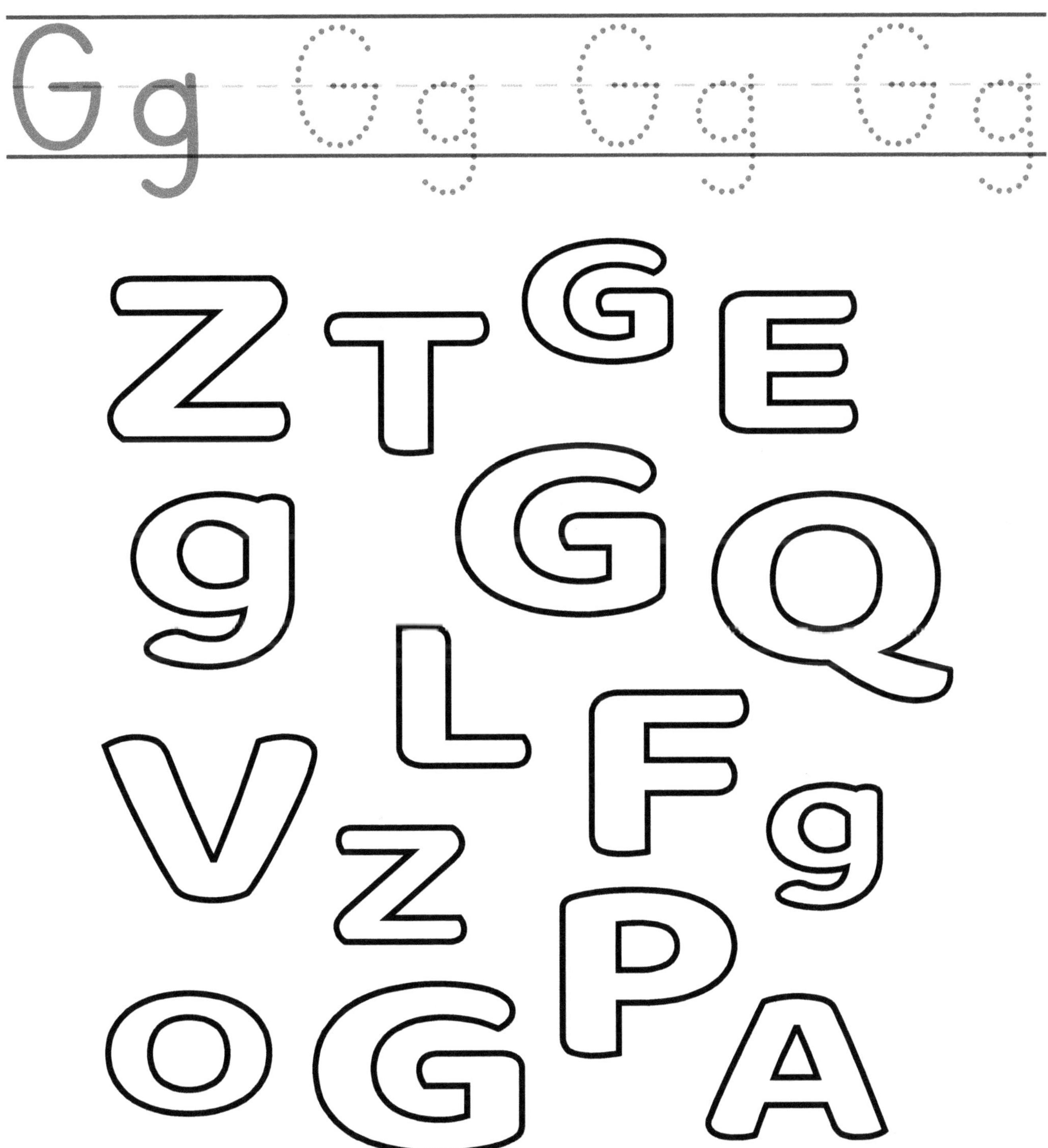

I Spy Letter

Highlight the uppercase and
lowercase that start with the letter you are learning.

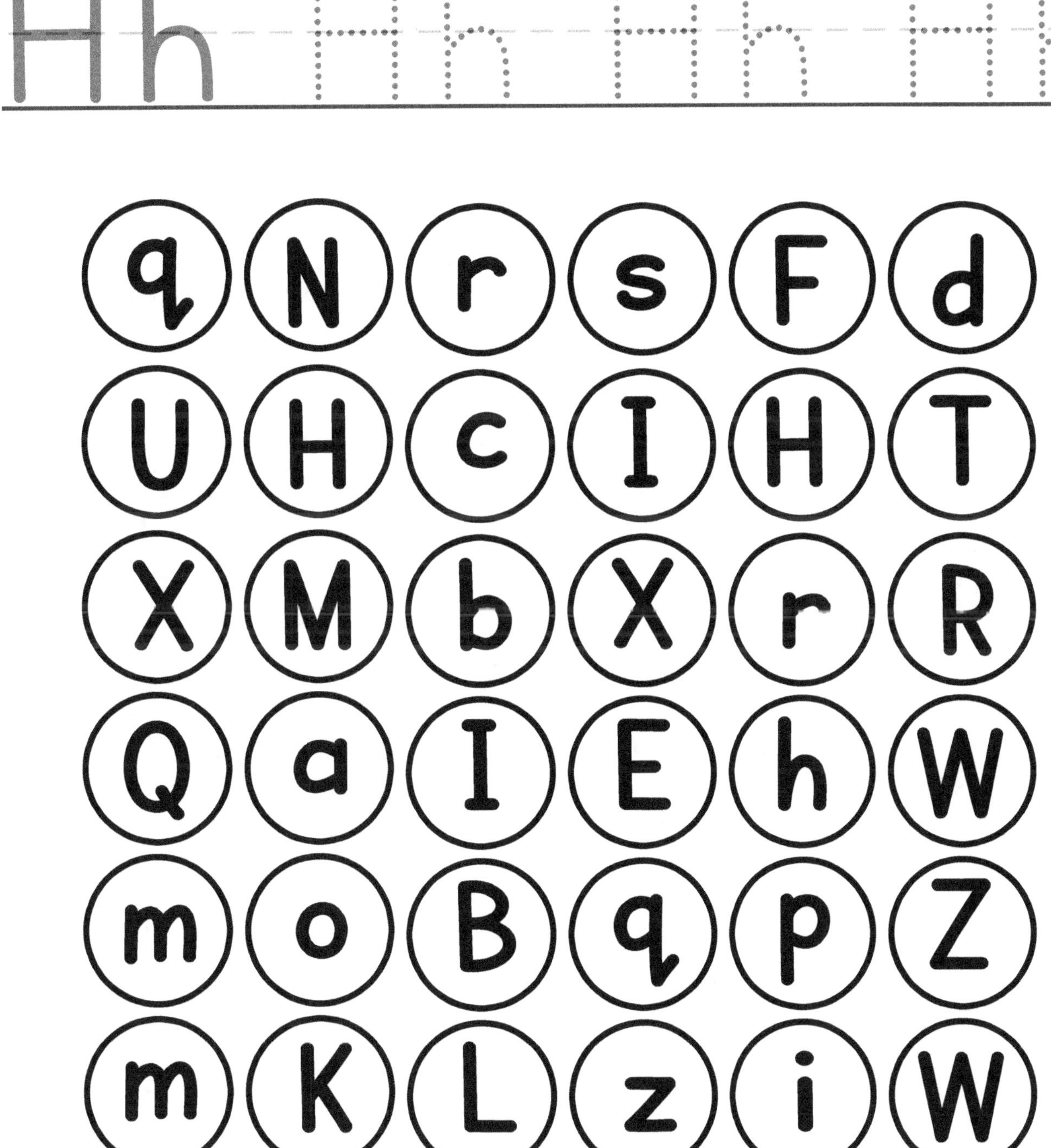

Letter Mazes

Highlight the uppercase and
lowercase that start with the letter you are learning.

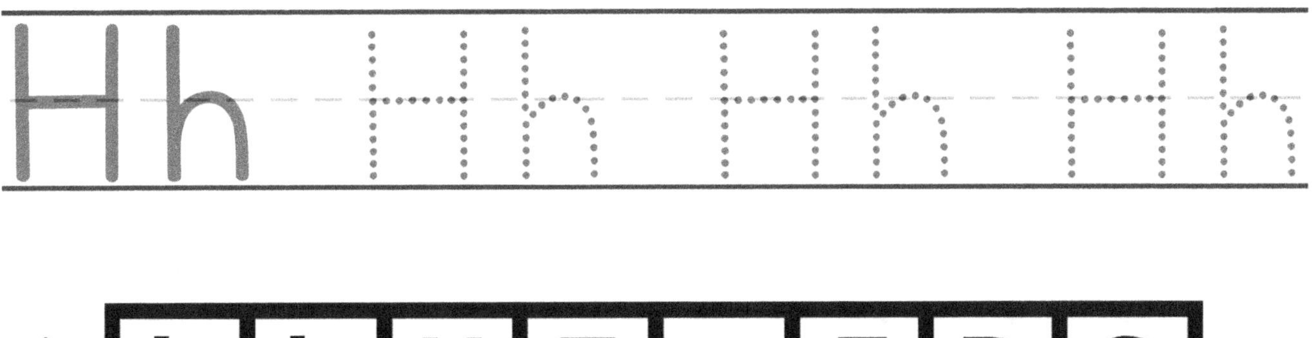

h	h	H	Z	a	F	D	S
r	n	h	R	7	h	h	h
k	H	H	t	b	H	R	H
Y	h	f	k	Q	h	E	H
E	h	m	H	h	h	N	H
B	H	H	h	U	u	S	h
D	o	E	V	E	c	o	H
f	l	r	C	N	t	J	h

Find the Letter

Highlight the uppercase and
lowercase that start with the letter you are learning.

I Spy Letter

Highlight the uppercase and
lowercase that start with the letter you are learning.

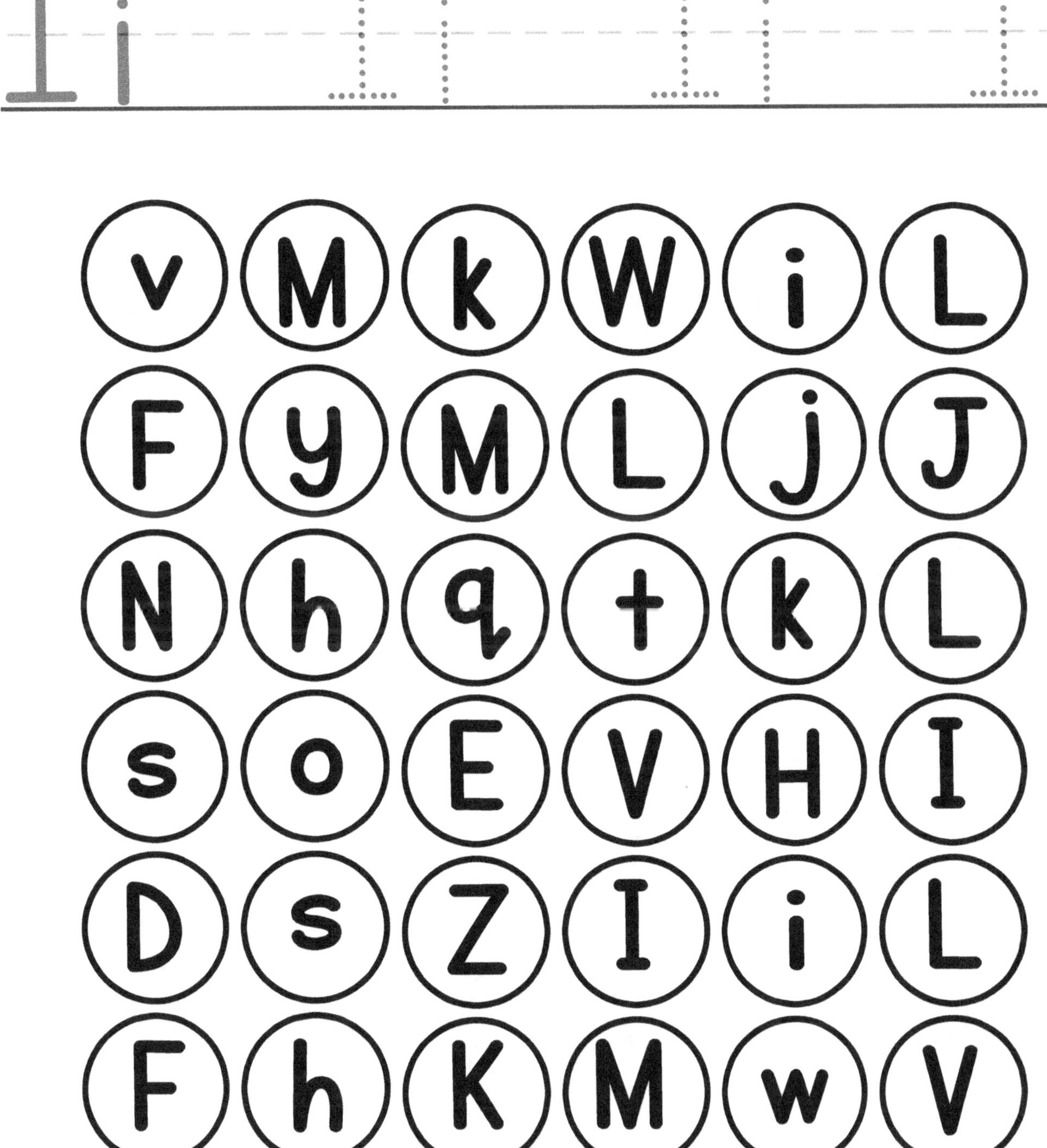

Letter Mazes

Highlight the uppercase and
lowercase that start with the letter you are learning.

I	i	r	i	I	I	i	h
e	i	Y	i	q	o	i	d
M	i	I	i	b	t	i	b
o	4	l	k	I	I	I	U
R	u	f	g	i	C	N	v
E	i	i	I	i	o	S	l
w	I	E	W	V	N	H	j
H	i	I	I	i	i	i	I

Find the Letter

Highlight the uppercase and
lowercase that start with the letter you are learning.

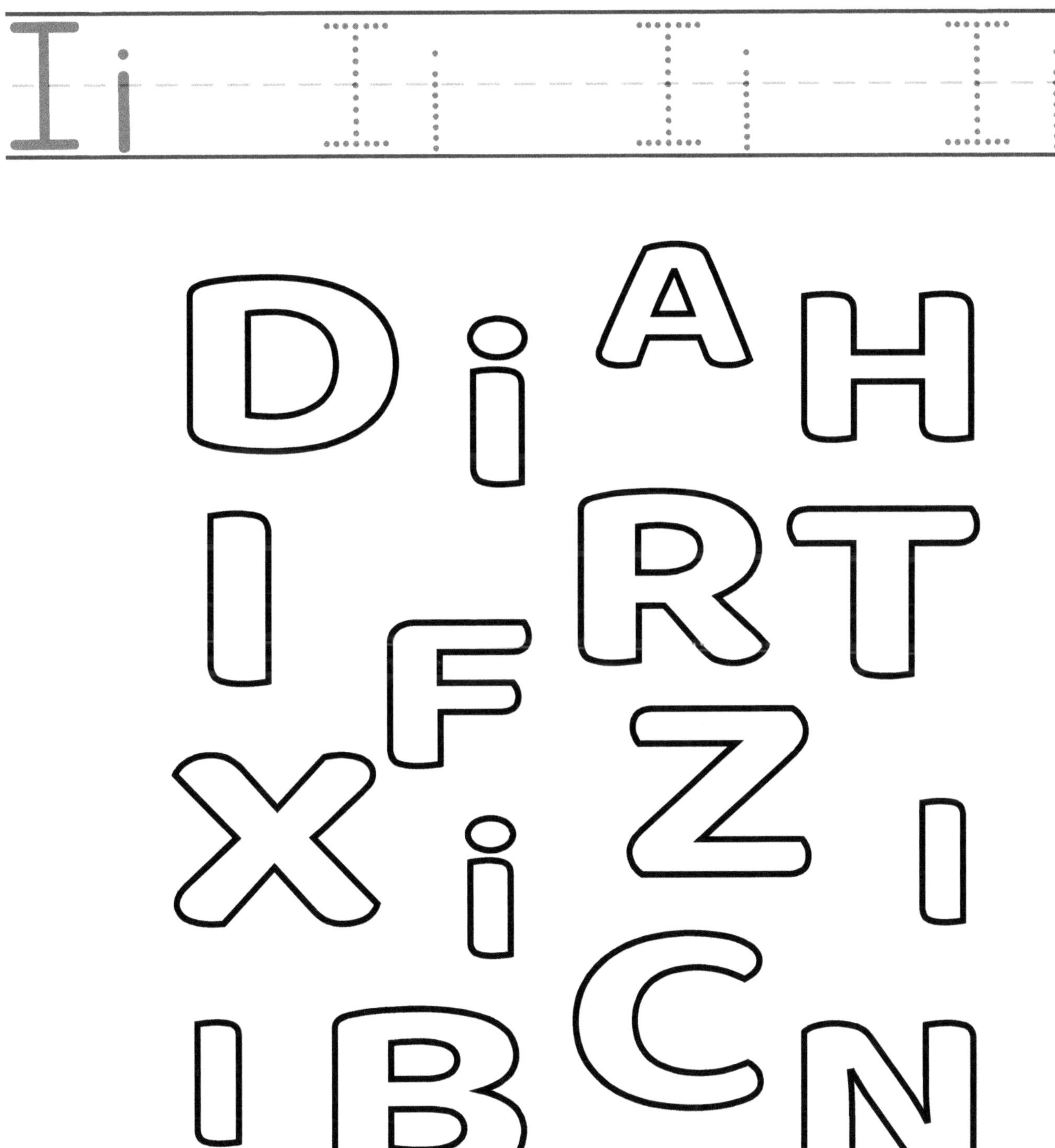

I Spy Letter

Highlight the uppercase and
lowercase that start with the letter you are learning.

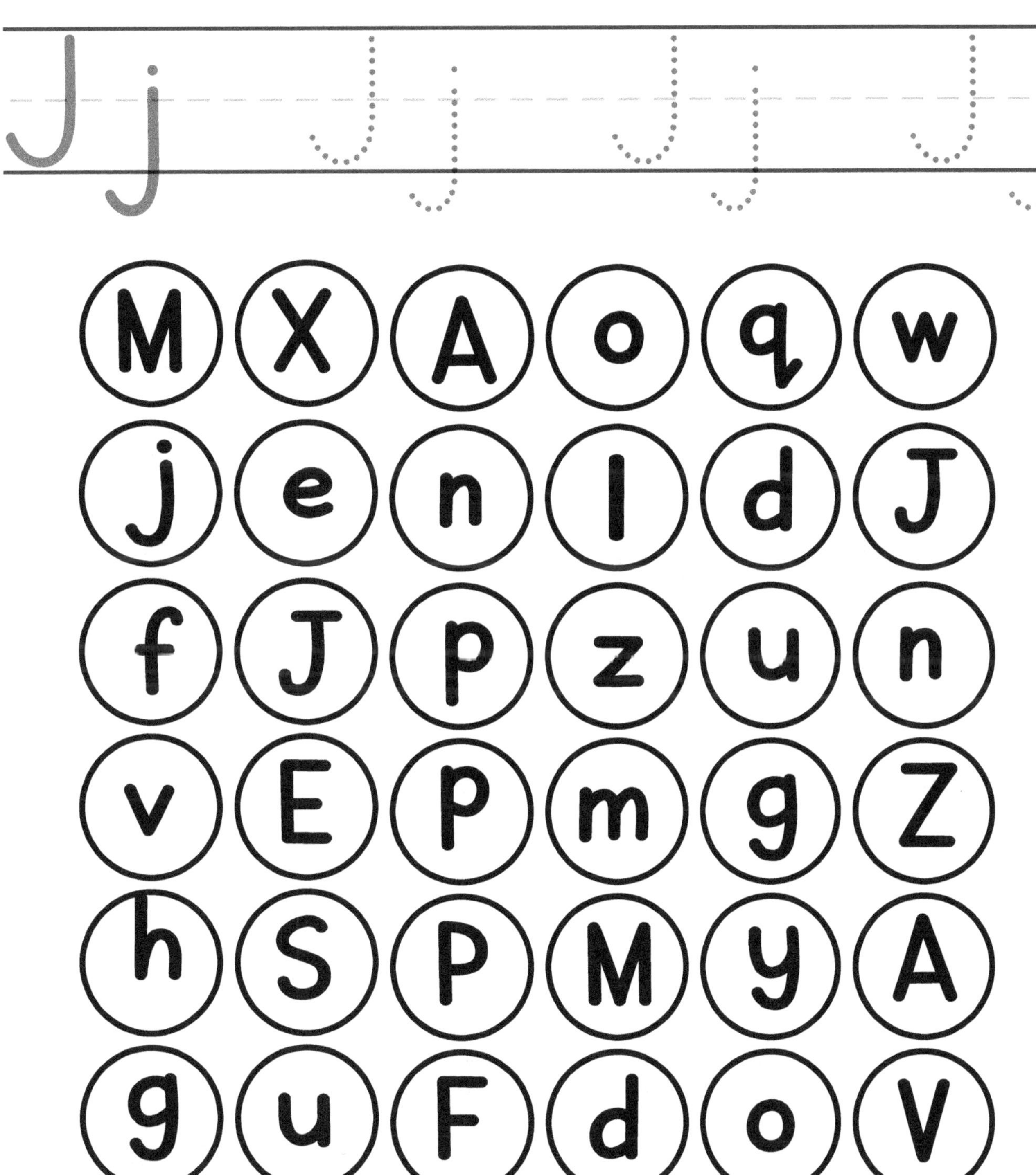

Letter Mazes

Highlight the uppercase and
lowercase that start with the letter you are learning.

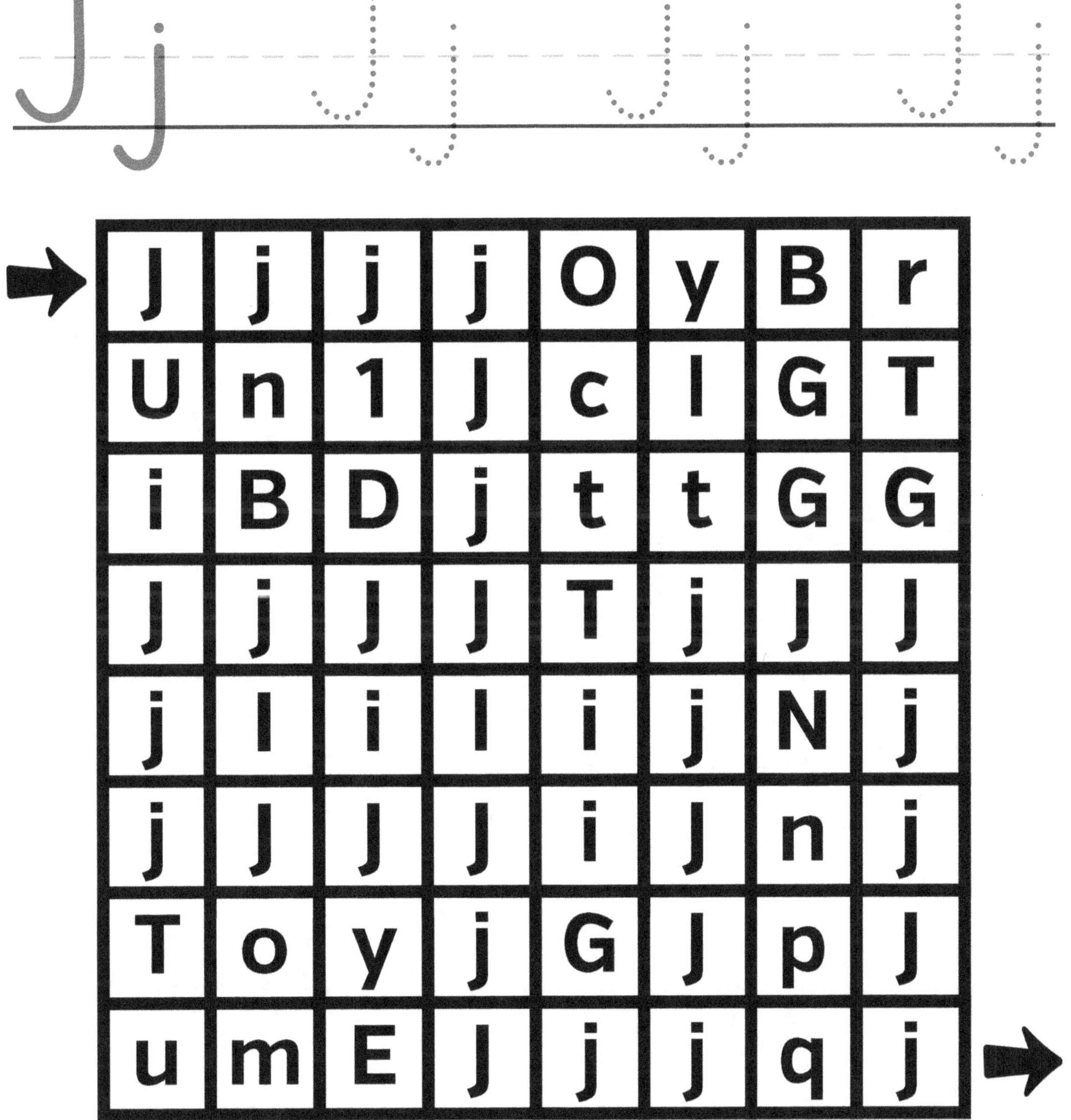

Find the Letter

Highlight the uppercase and
lowercase that start with the letter you are learning.

I Spy Letter

Highlight the uppercase and
lowercase that start with the letter you are learning.

K k

Letter Mazes

Highlight the uppercase and
lowercase that start with the letter you are learning.

Kk Kk Kk Kk

K	k	k	K	Q	O	i	B
b	C	X	k	q	I	T	y
U	o	D	k	b	K	K	k
E	M	I	k	Q	K	E	k
v	b	c	k	K	k	U	k
E	Z	X	n	B	o	Y	K
J	o	E	W	9	N	p	k
j	Y	b	R	c	E	q	K

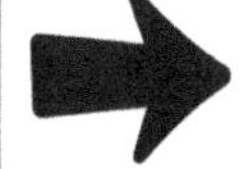

Find the Letter

Highlight the uppercase and
lowercase that start with the letter you are learning.

I Spy Letter

Highlight the uppercase and
lowercase that start with the letter you are learning.

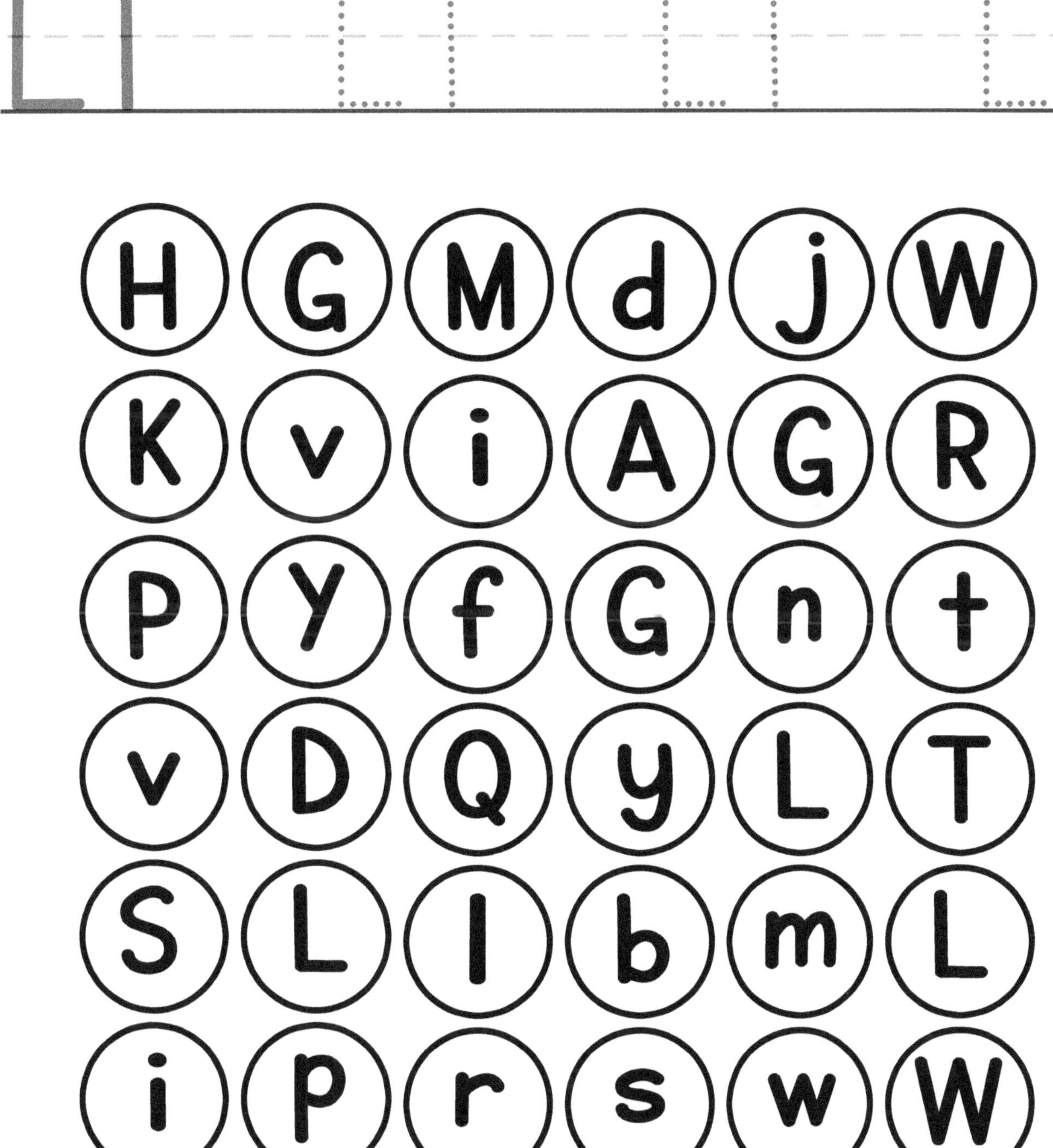

Letter Mazes

Highlight the uppercase and
lowercase that start with the letter you are learning.

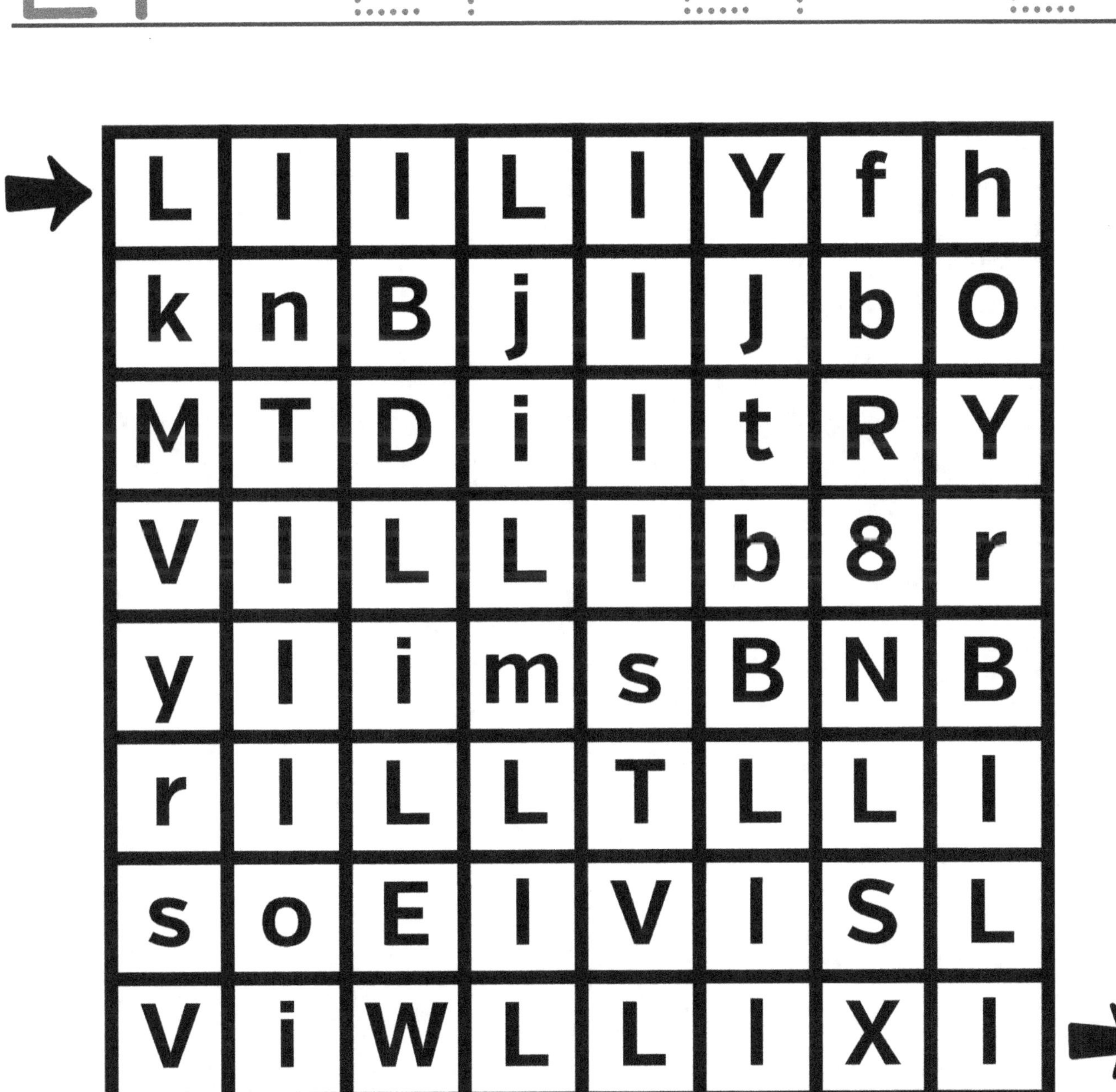

Find the Letter

Highlight the uppercase and
lowercase that start with the letter you are learning.

I Spy Letter

Highlight the uppercase and
lowercase that start with the letter you are learning.

M m   M m   M m   M m

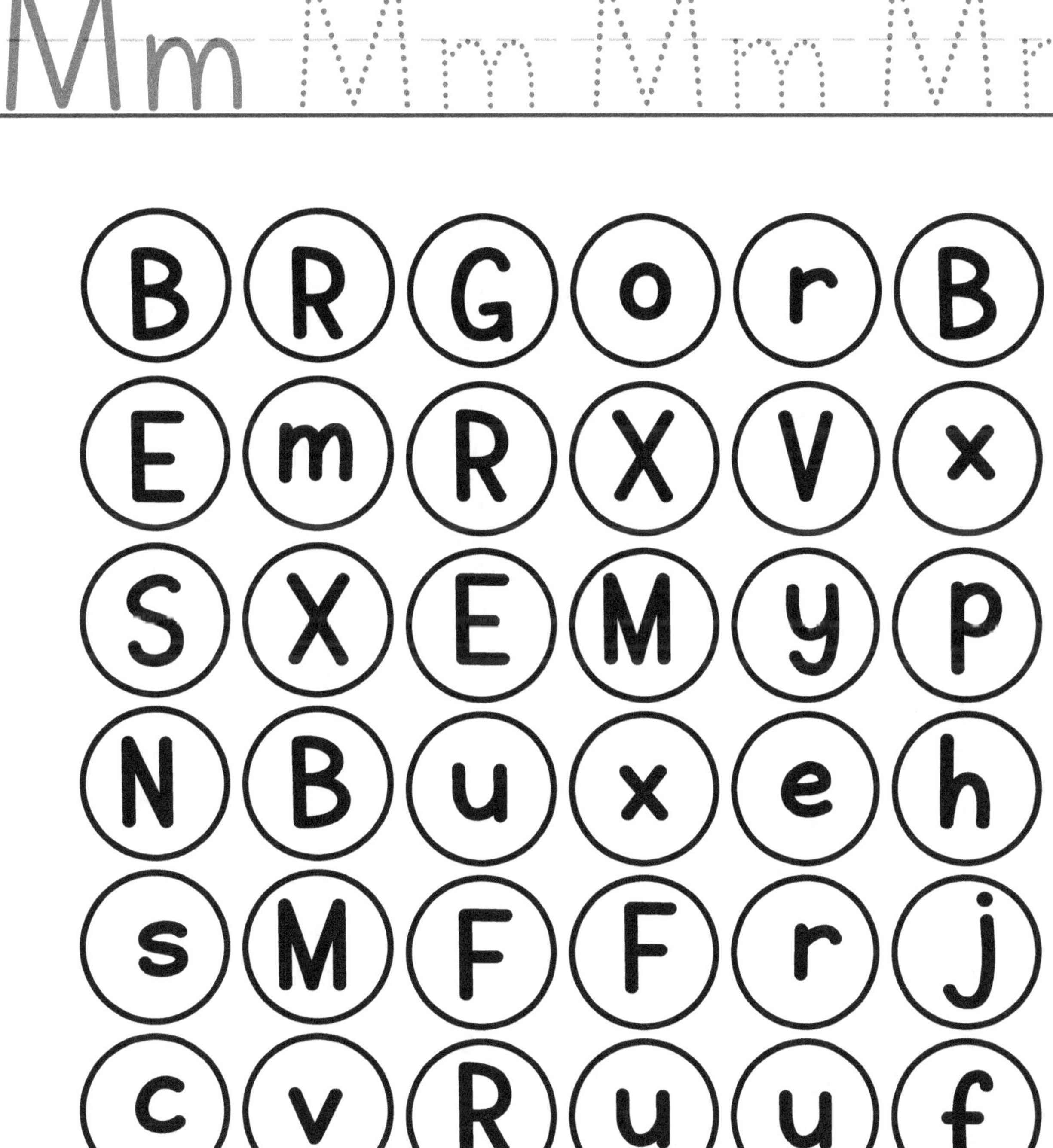

Letter Mazes

Highlight the uppercase and
lowercase that start with the letter you are learning.

Mm Mm Mm Mm

M	c	M	m	M	n	D	P
m	n	m	R	m	m	m	g
M	w	m	d	b	t	M	o
m	m	M	k	w	w	M	M
b	n	3	l	n	B	N	m
u	Z	a	m	M	M	M	m
w	o	E	m	u	N	S	u
d	w	w	M	m	m	M	m

Find the Letter

Highlight the uppercase and
lowercase that start with the letter you are learning.

M m M m M m M m M m

D L m H
B M I
A
J F
M K
M Z S m

I Spy Letter

Highlight the uppercase and
lowercase that start with the letter you are learning.

N n Nn Nn Nn

Letter Mazes

Highlight the uppercase and
lowercase that start with the letter you are learning.

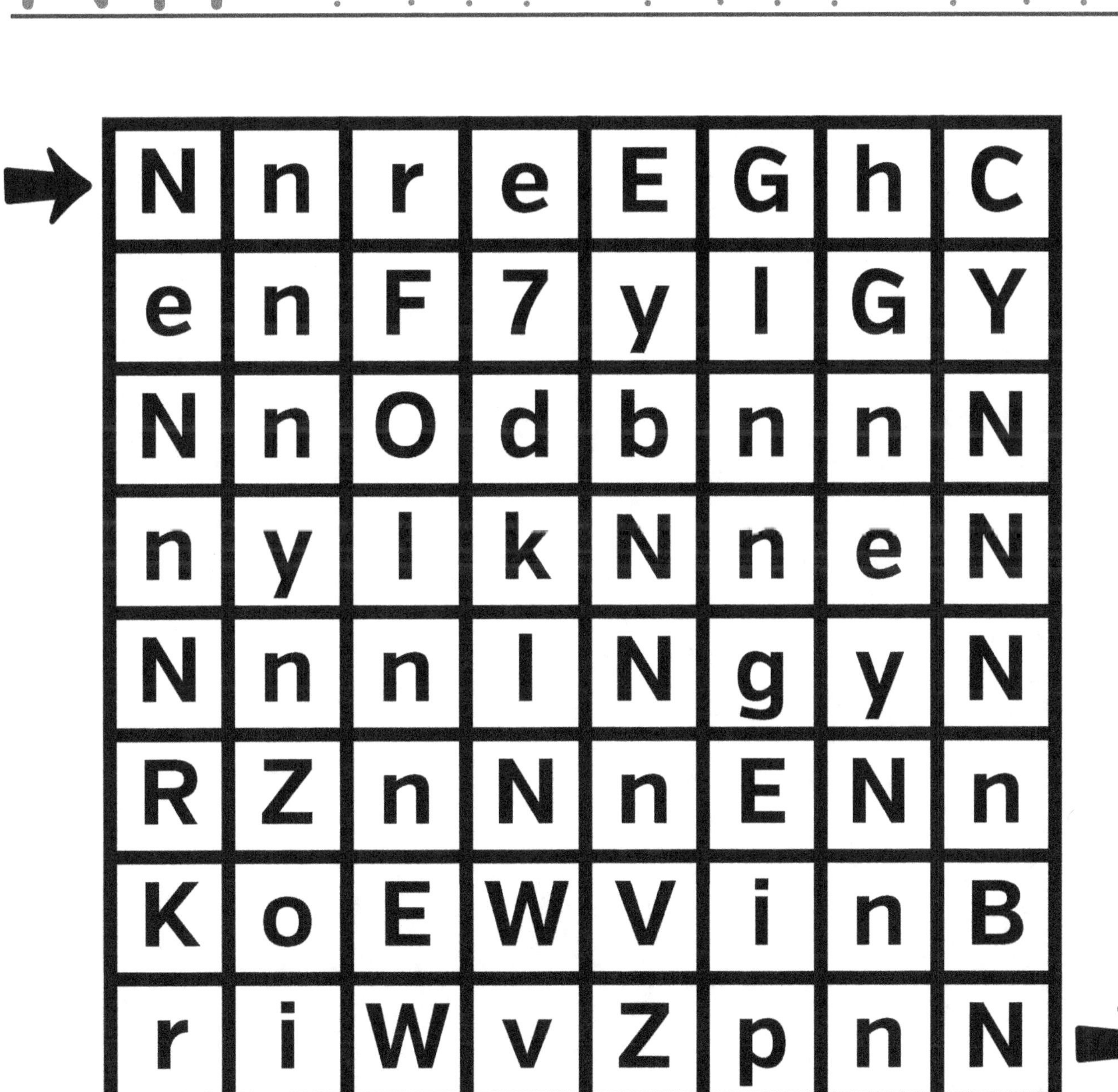

Find the Letter

Highlight the uppercase and
lowercase that start with the letter you are learning.

N n   N n   N n   N n

C n N V
P I
W P
Y N R
Y n
N A S M

I Spy Letter

Highlight the uppercase and
lowercase that start with the letter you are learning.

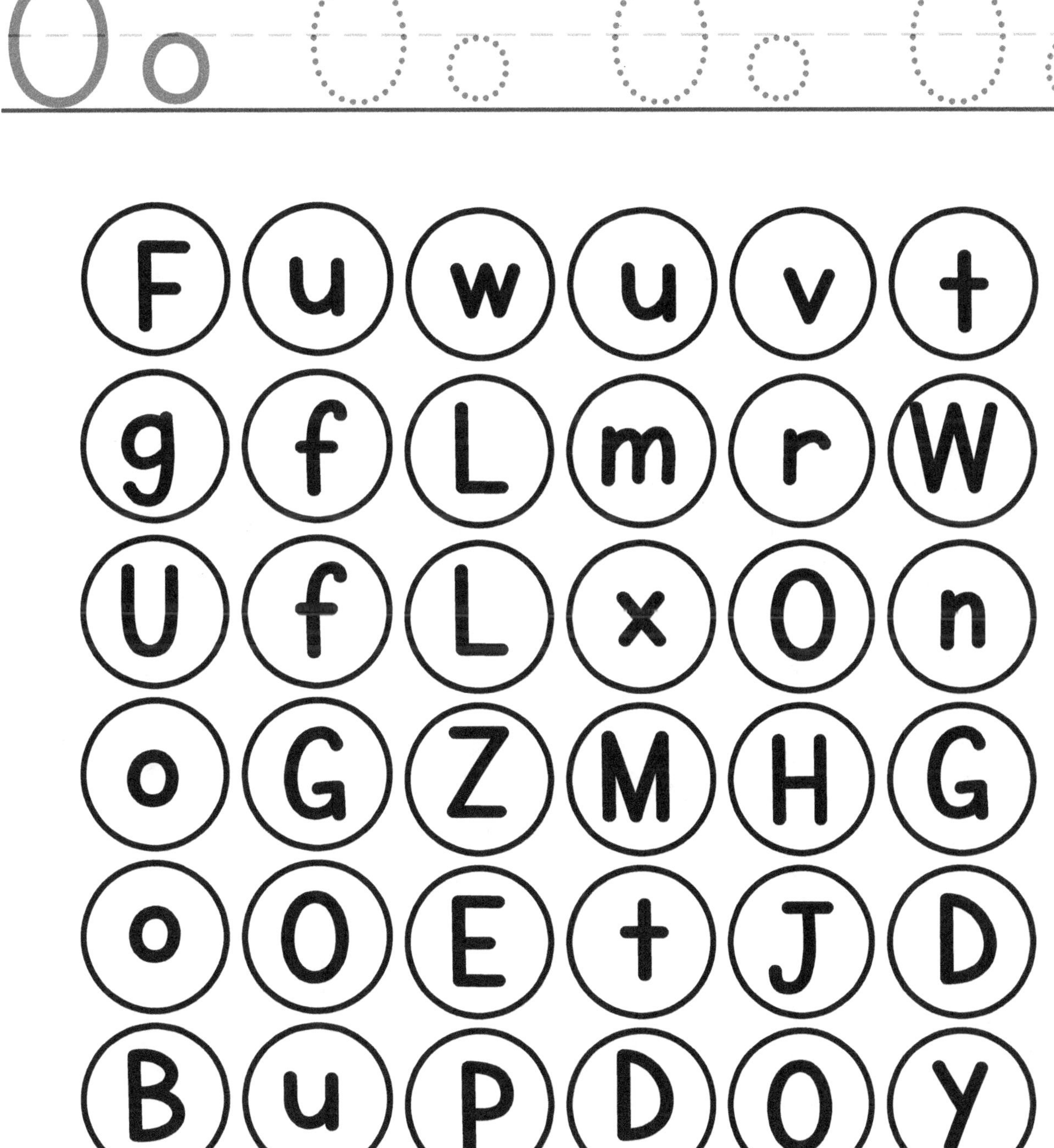

Letter Mazes

Highlight the uppercase and
lowercase that start with the letter you are learning.

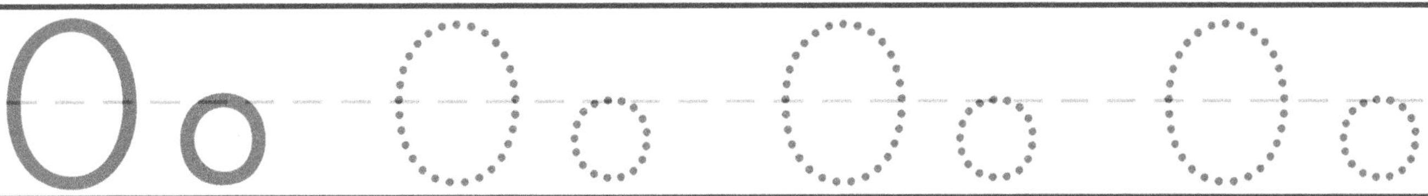

O	o	O	G	u	y	n	v
i	u	o	i	R	s	a	R
p	o	o	d	b	G	n	u
s	O	e	S	Q	O	o	o
c	O	o	o	m	O	N	o
Q	Z	8	O	o	o	S	o
Y	o	E	W	V	N	S	O
K	o	W	q	H	U	I	O

Find the Letter

Highlight the uppercase and
lowercase that start with the letter you are learning.

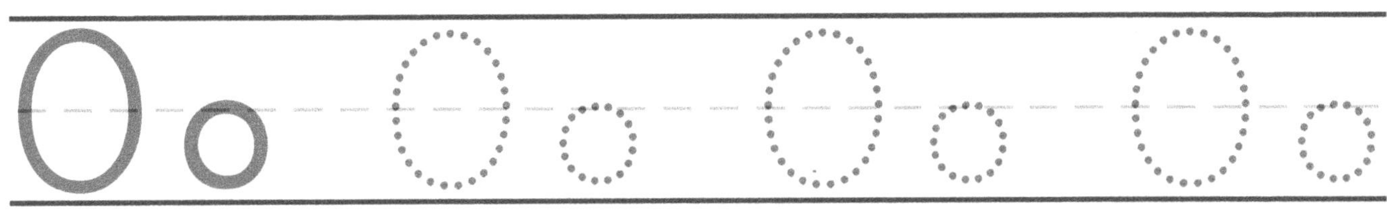

C F O O Q
O A O R
Z A W O K
O B Y G

I Spy Letter

Highlight the uppercase and
lowercase that start with the letter you are learning.

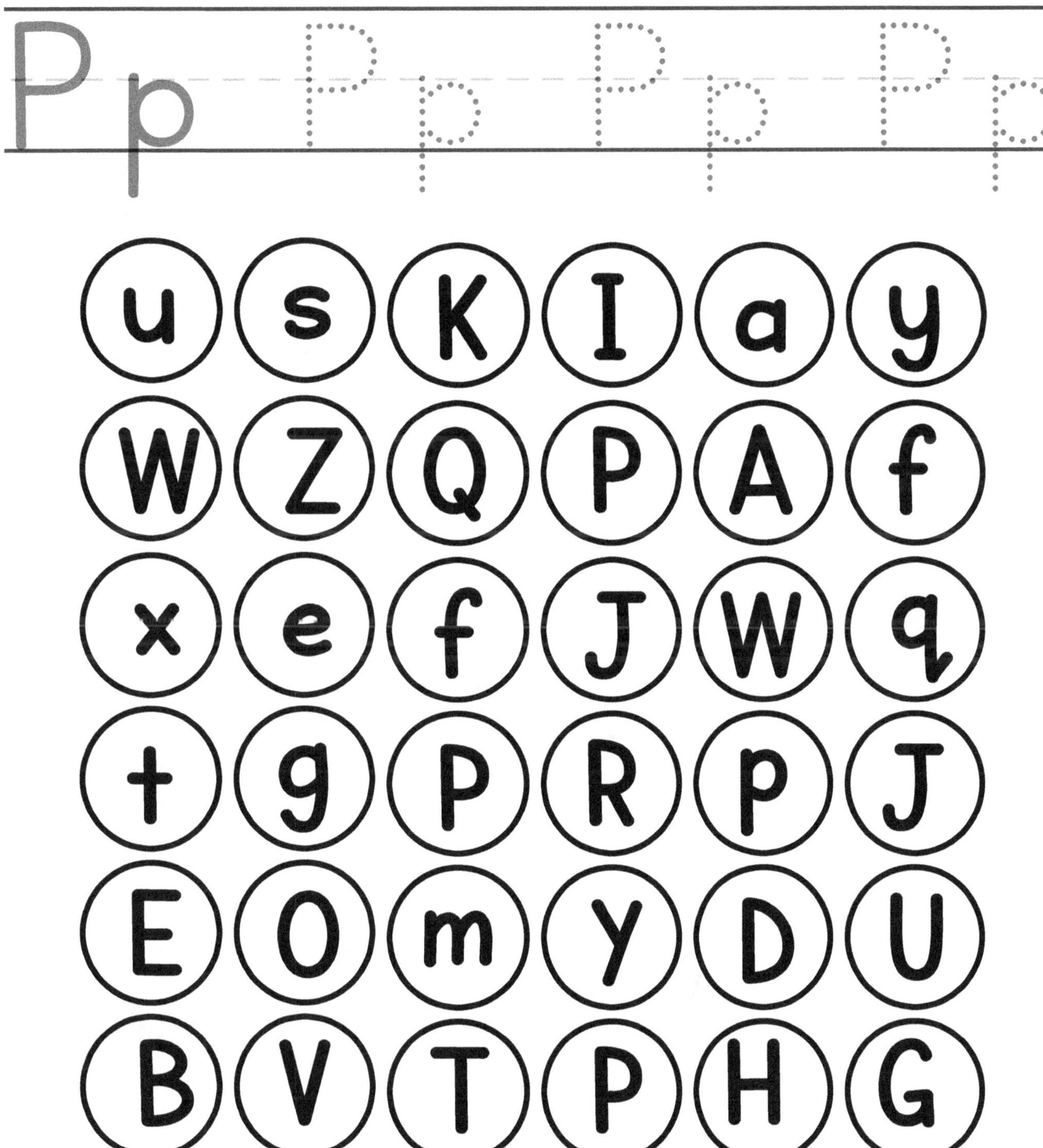

Letter Mazes

Highlight the uppercase and
lowercase that start with the letter you are learning.

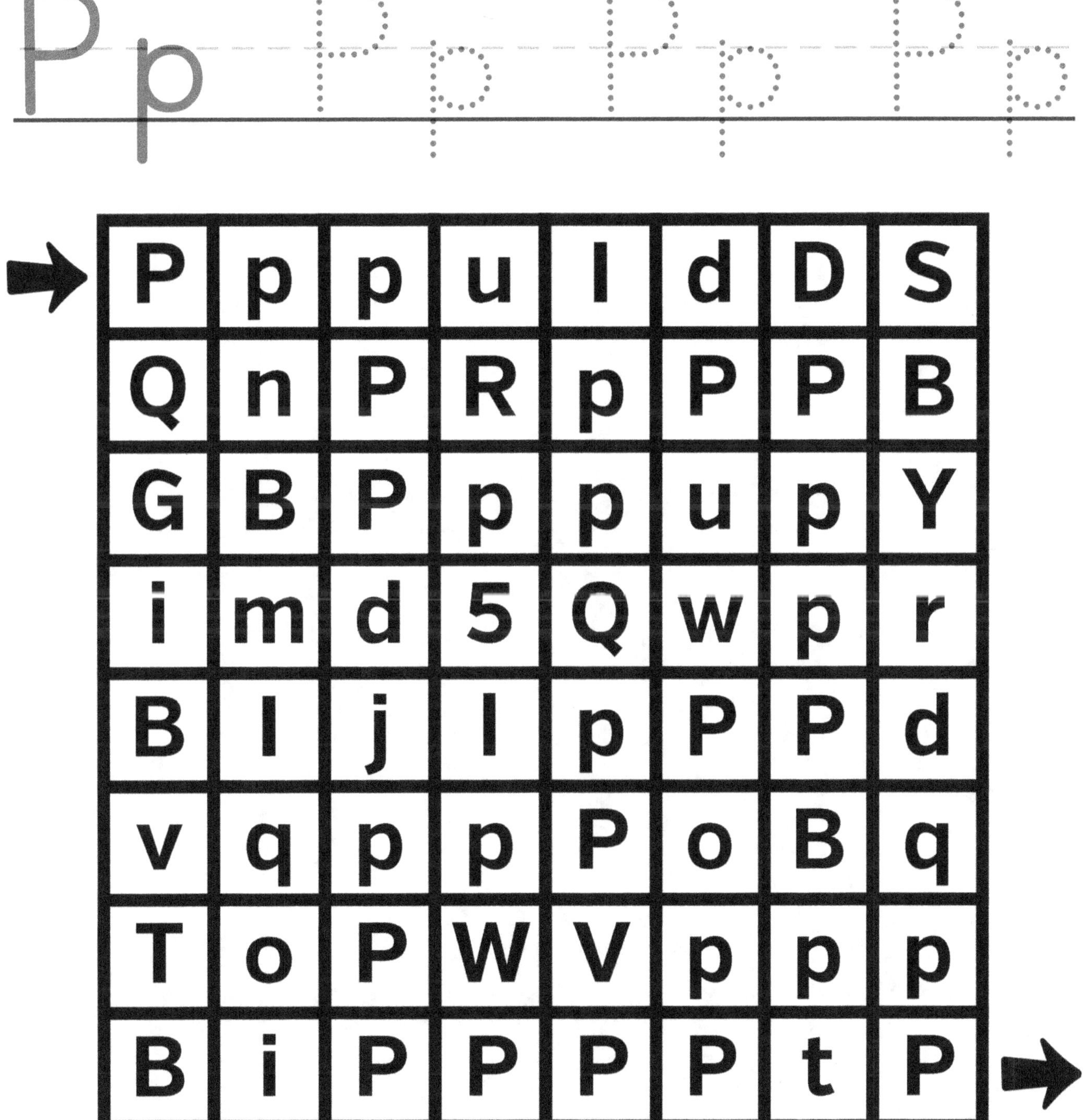

Find the Letter

Highlight the uppercase and
lowercase that start with the letter you are learning.

I Spy Letter

Highlight the uppercase and
lowercase that start with the letter you are learning.

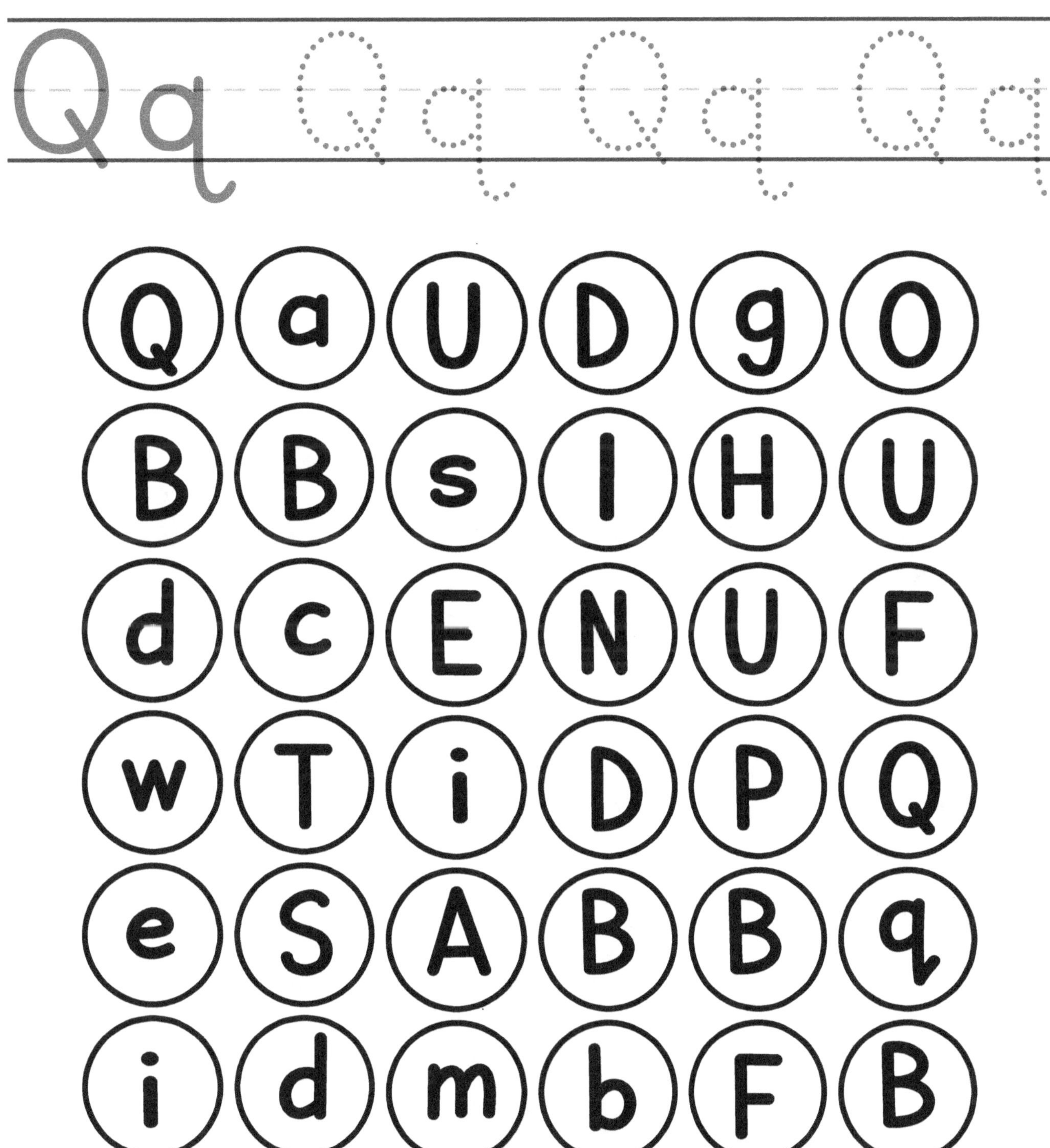

Letter Mazes

Highlight the uppercase and
lowercase that start with the letter you are learning.

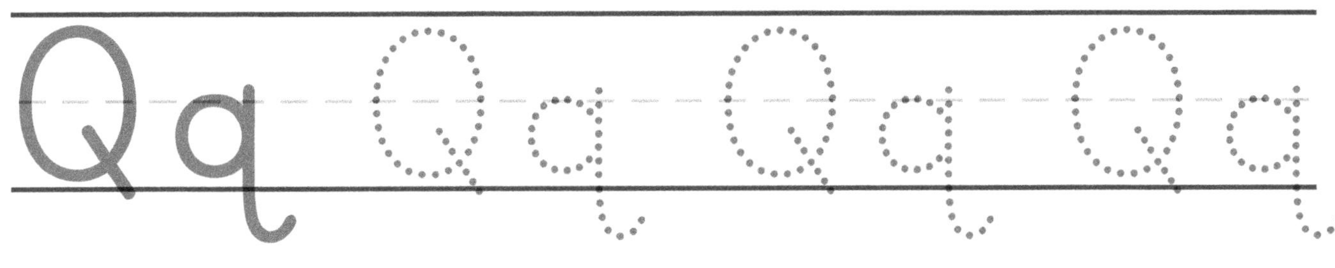

q	p	B	N	E	Q	Q	q
Q	d	Q	Q	q	Q	t	q
Q	p	Q	d	b	Y	R	Q
q	9	q	q	Q	Y	E	Q
q	o	i	l	q	B	q	q
Q	q	a	q	Q	o	Q	p
W	Q	E	q	O	N	q	u
O	q	Q	Q	E	I	Q	q

Find the Letter

Highlight the uppercase and
lowercase that start with the letter you are learning.

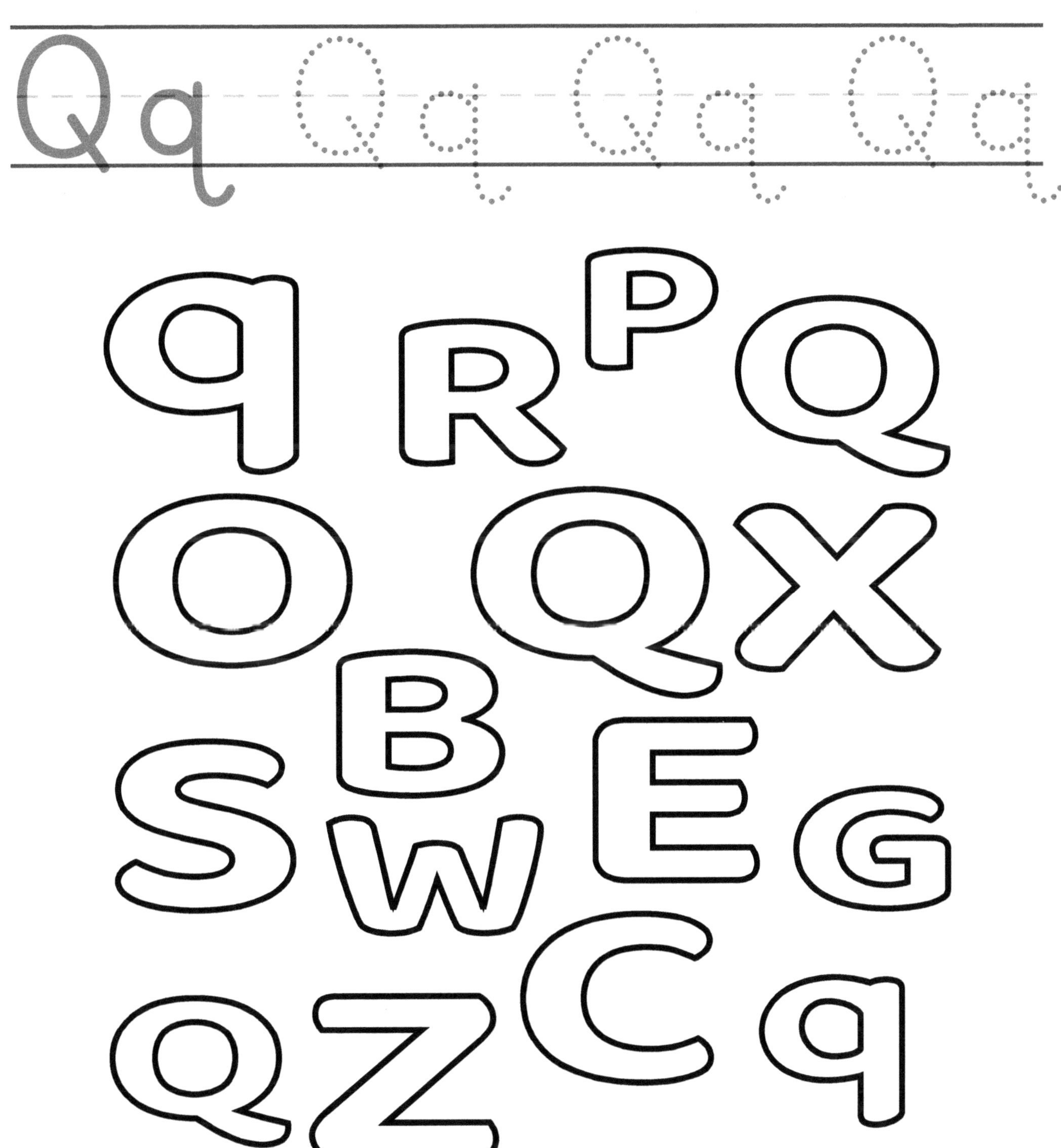

I Spy Letter

Highlight the uppercase and
lowercase that start with the letter you are learning.

Letter Mazes

Highlight the uppercase and
lowercase that start with the letter you are learning.

Rr Rr Rr Rr

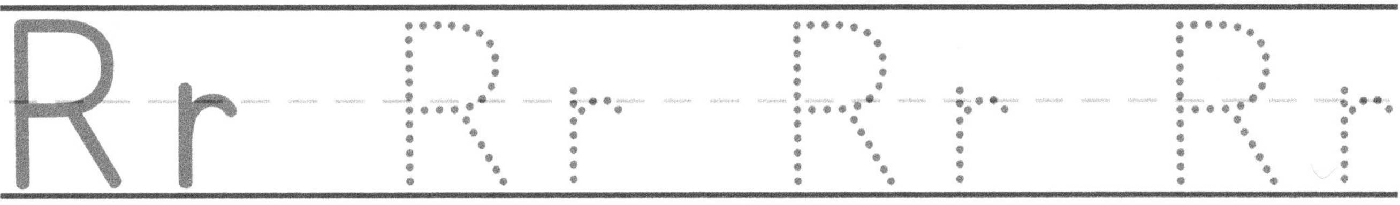

R	r	l	b	E	C	m	c
k	r	g	R	R	r	G	i
b	R	r	r	l	r	h	D
E	m	f	C	Q	R	E	u
l	m	i	R	R	R	N	f
c	r	r	r	f	o	S	M
M	R	E	K	p	R	r	R
2	R	R	r	R	R	P	r

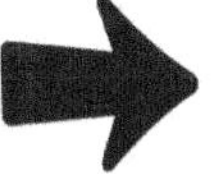

Find the Letter

Highlight the uppercase and
lowercase that start with the letter you are learning.

R r R r R r R r

I Spy Letter

Highlight the uppercase and
lowercase that start with the letter you are learning.

Letter Mazes

Highlight the uppercase and
lowercase that start with the letter you are learning.

S s S s S s S s

S	Y	r	v	E	W	J	k
s	g	f	R	d	l	4	Y
s	v	X	d	b	t	R	h
s	m	S	s	s	s	S	c
S	I	S	I	m	B	s	s
S	S	s	v	s	s	S	e
f	o	U	r	S	N	y	O
K	E	c	k	S	S	s	S

Find the Letter

Highlight the uppercase and
lowercase that start with the letter you are learning.

S s S s S s S s

I Spy Letter

Highlight the uppercase and
lowercase that start with the letter you are learning.

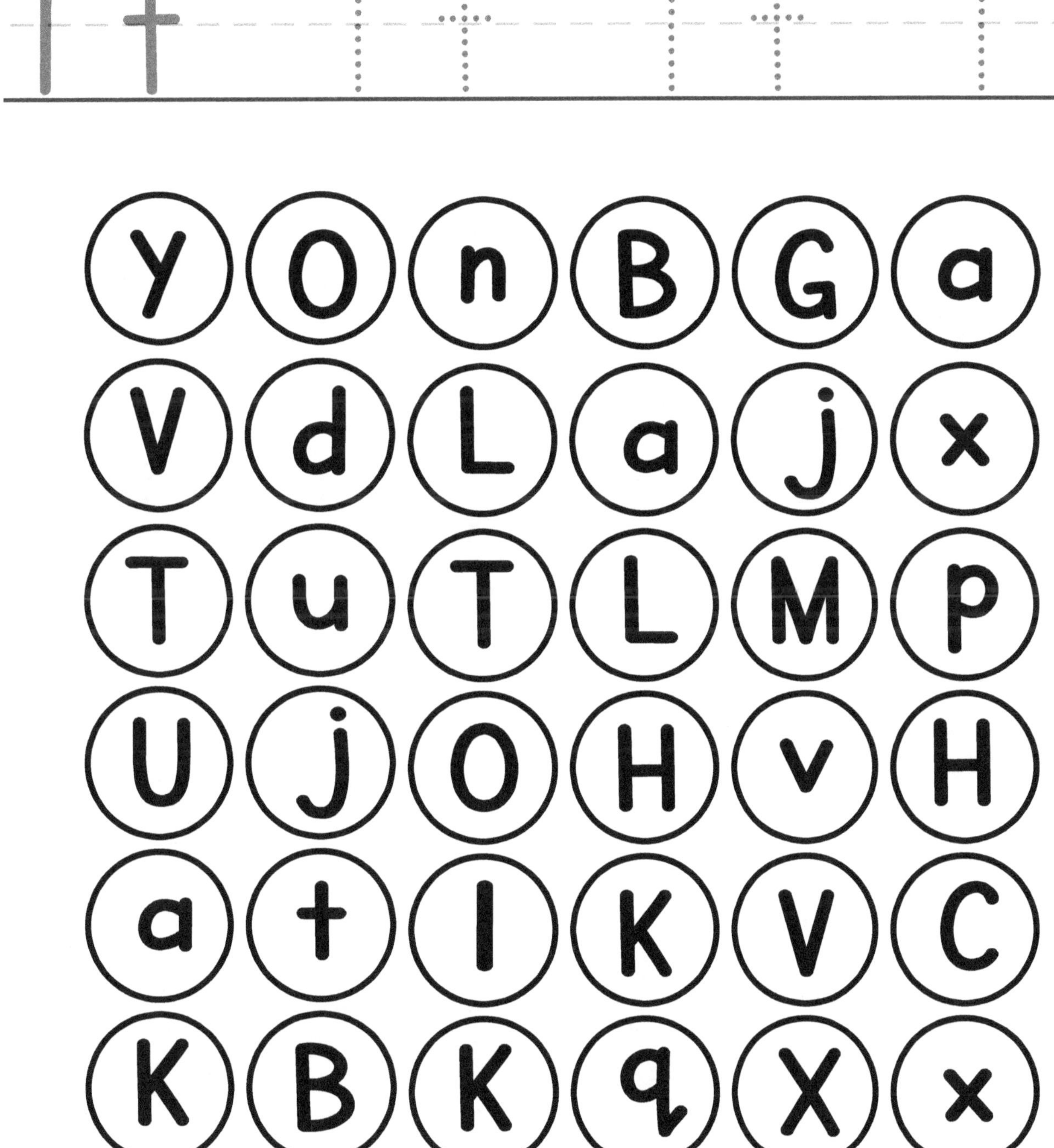

Letter Mazes

Highlight the uppercase and
lowercase that start with the letter you are learning.

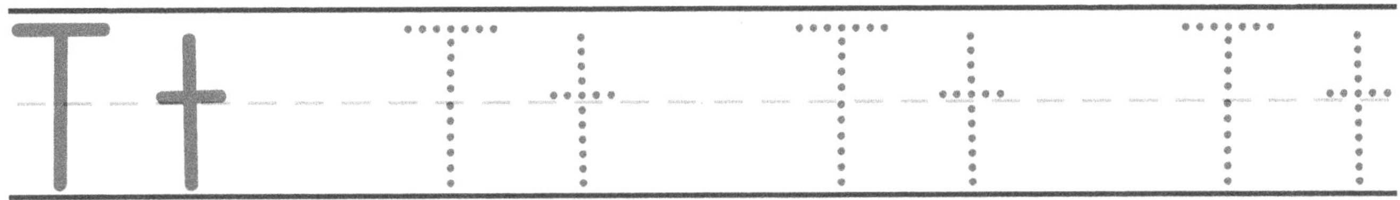

T	t	t	T	t	t	n	B
J	n	B	v	q	T	n	M
f	B	T	t	T	t	t	k
E	W	t	k	d	w	E	t
v	I	T	t	m	B	N	e
Q	R	z	t	T	t	S	E
1	9	O	E	r	T	S	V
o	i	s	y	y	T	T	T

Find the Letter

Highlight the uppercase and
lowercase that start with the letter you are learning.

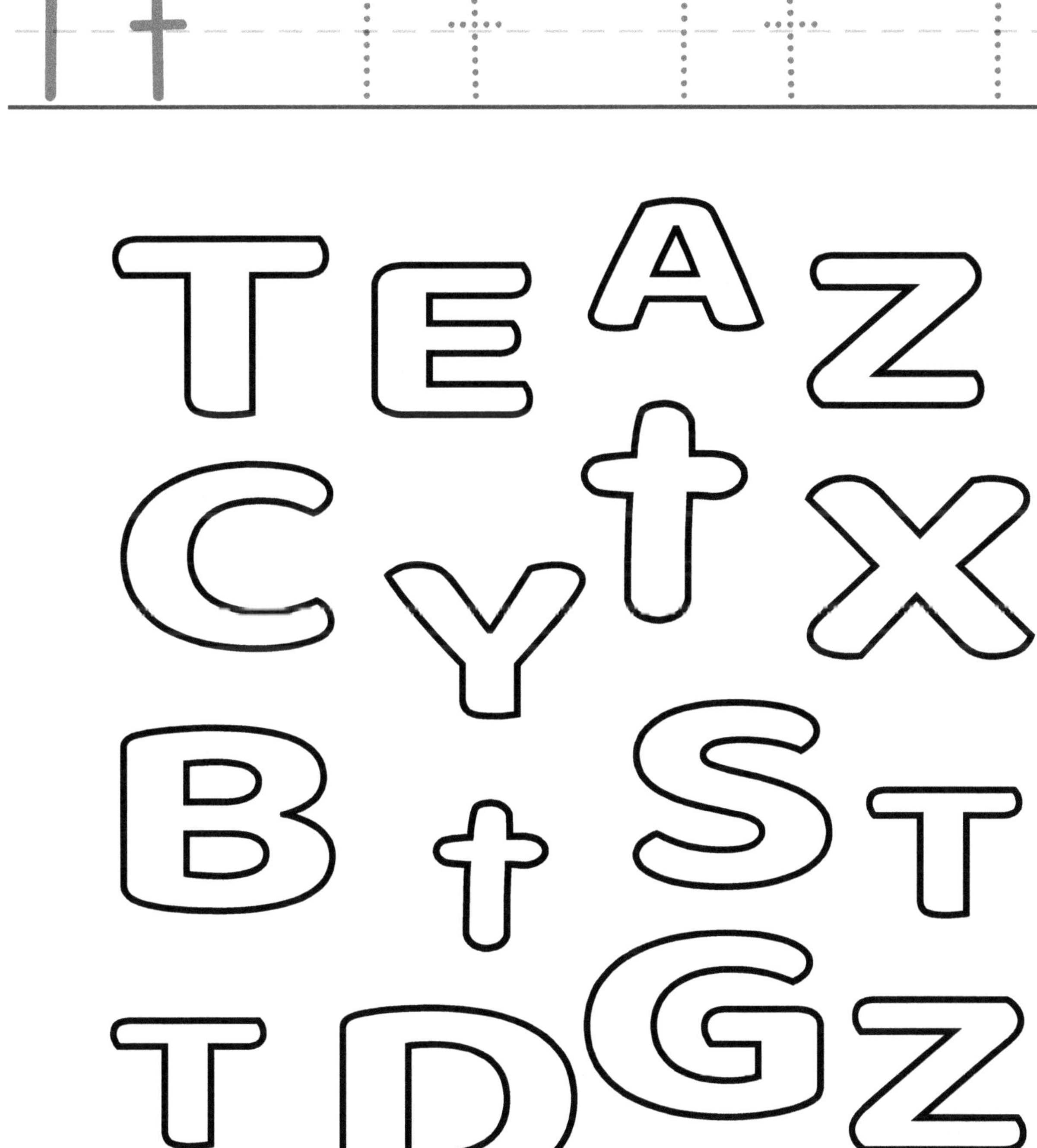

I Spy Letter

Highlight the uppercase and
lowercase that start with the letter you are learning.

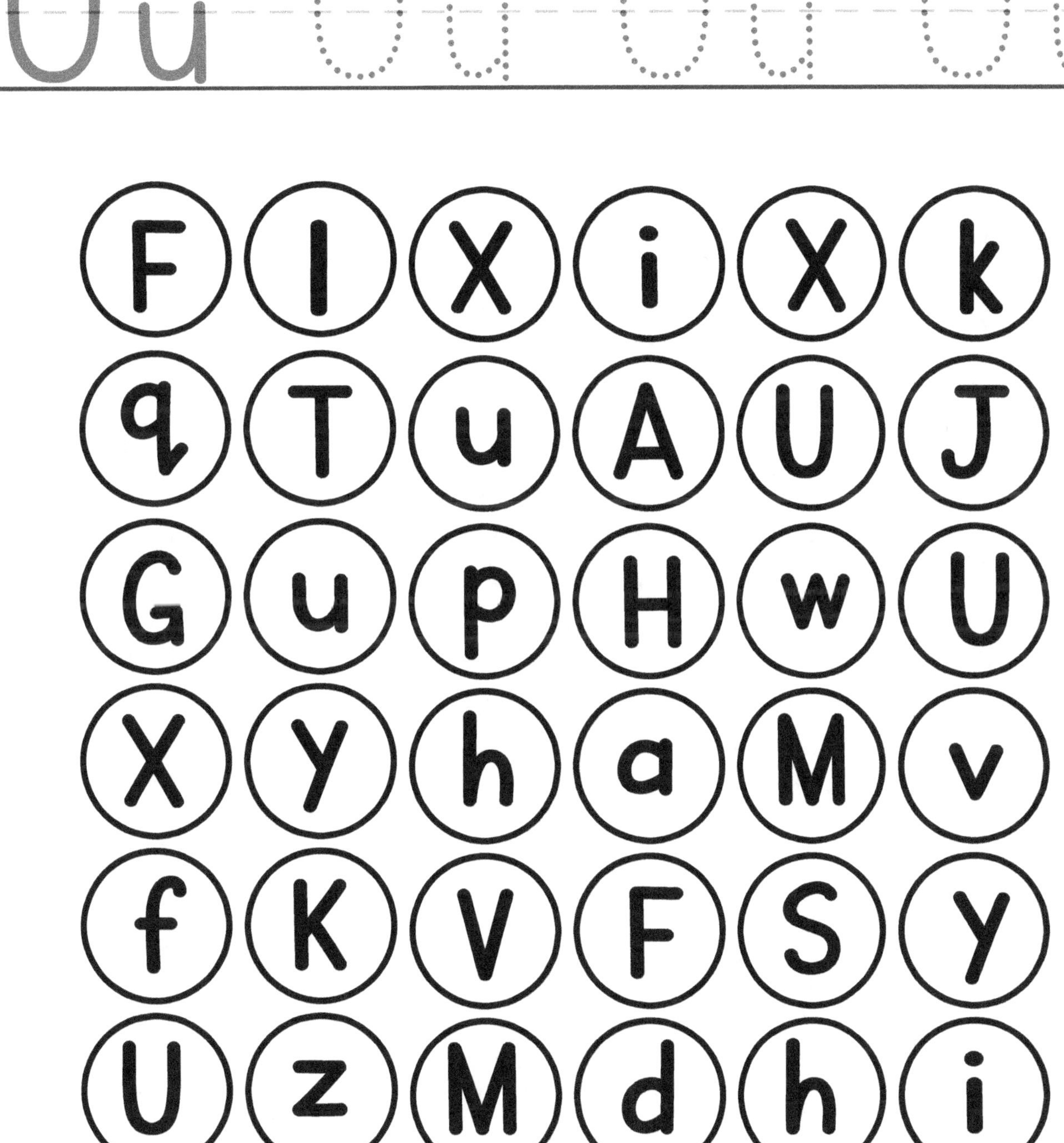

Letter Mazes

Highlight the uppercase and
lowercase that start with the letter you are learning.

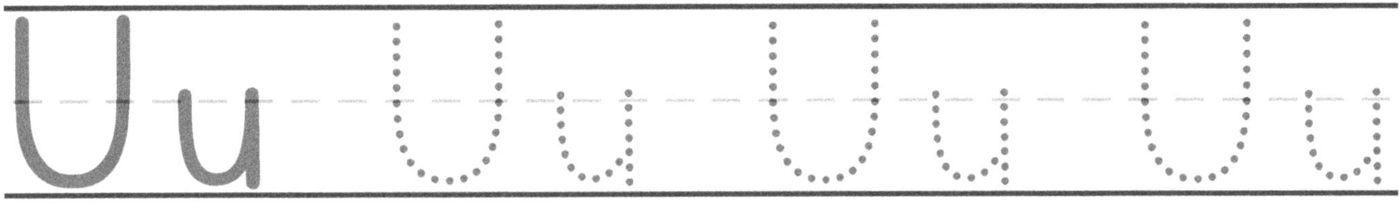

U	u	u	U	e	N	C	i
t	v	m	u	q	l	G	F
D	G	y	U	U	U	U	r
i	p	l	k	Q	w	U	u
B	U	U	u	m	B	N	u
6	u	Y	U	u	u	U	u
C	u	p	l	z	o	r	K
I	U	U	U	u	U	u	u

Find the Letter

Highlight the uppercase and
lowercase that start with the letter you are learning.

U u

I Spy Letter

Highlight the uppercase and
lowercase that start with the letter you are learning.

V v

Letter Mazes

Highlight the uppercase and
lowercase that start with the letter you are learning.

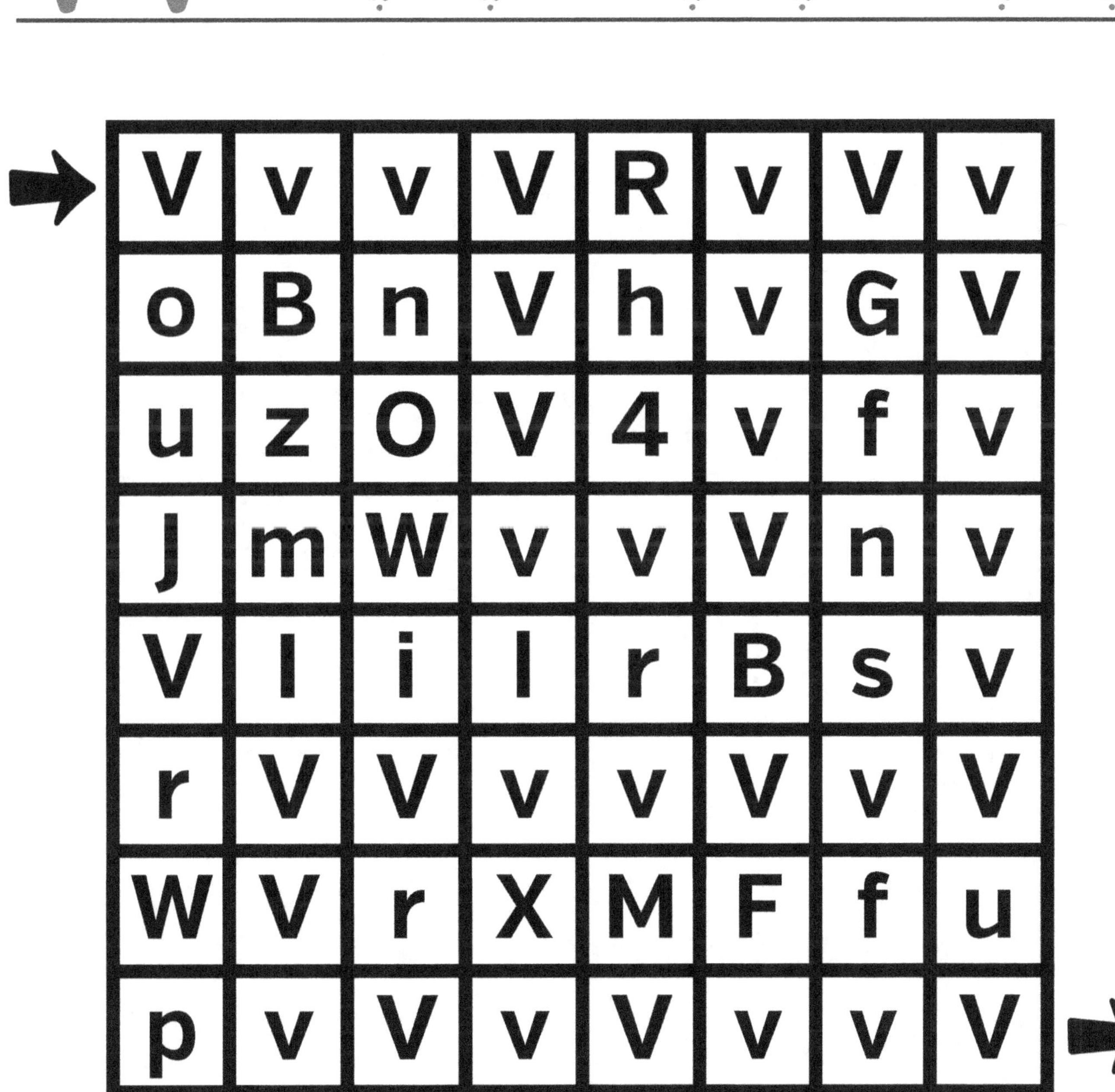

Find the Letter

Highlight the uppercase and
lowercase that start with the letter you are learning.

V v

I Spy Letter

Highlight the uppercase and
lowercase that start with the letter you are learning.

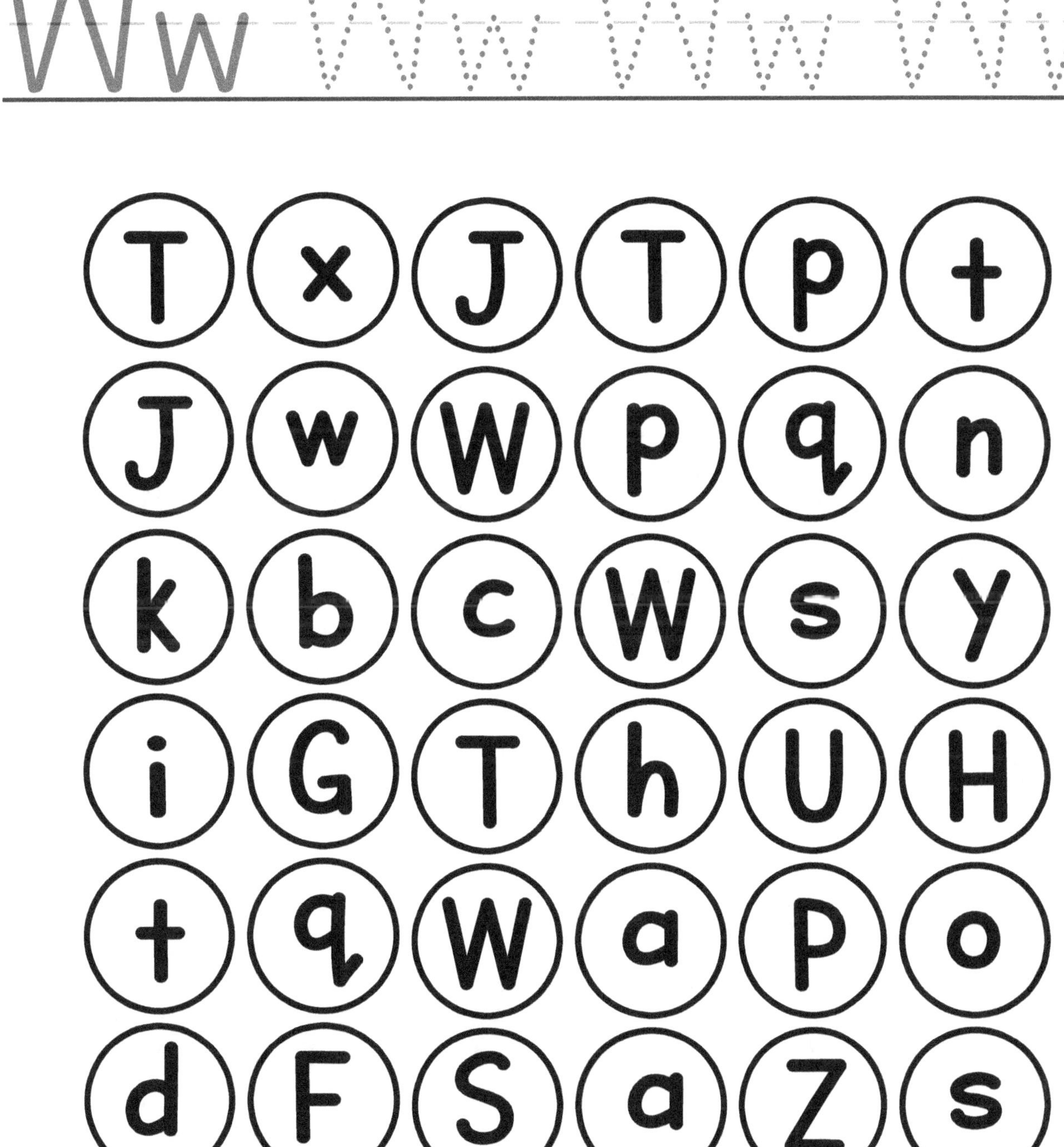

Letter Mazes

Highlight the uppercase and
lowercase that start with the letter you are learning.

Ww Ww Ww Ww

W	W	w	w	W	g	P	d
e	B	c	d	w	l	G	W
M	t	w	w	W	t	R	V
o	i	W	u	v	w	E	V
w	w	w	l	m	W	W	W
w	s	a	C	u	w	S	w
w	o	2	W	W	w	S	w
W	w	W	w	e	q	c	w

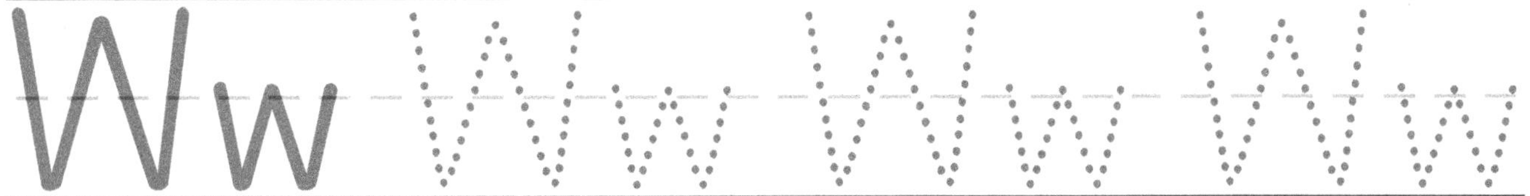

Find the Letter

Highlight the uppercase and
lowercase that start with the letter you are learning.

Ww

W X w

F

U w A

Q

J E

w K

B C Y w

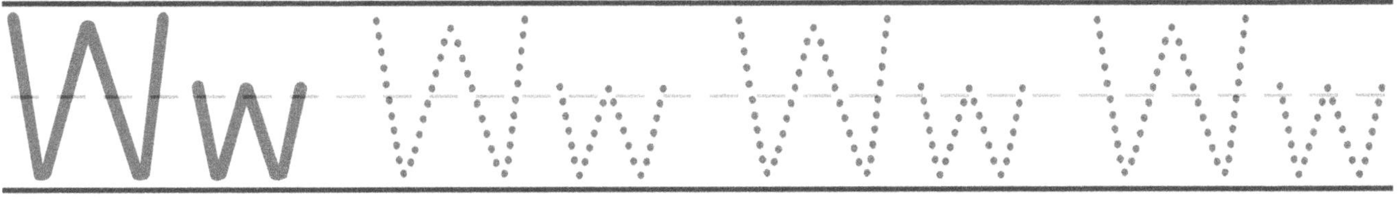

I Spy Letter

Highlight the uppercase and
lowercase that start with the letter you are learning.

Letter Mazes

Highlight the uppercase and
lowercase that start with the letter you are learning.

| X | x | | X | x | | X | x | | X | x |

x	f	X	x	x	C	P	s
x	y	x	u	x	l	5	B
x	K	X	B	X	x	X	x
x	l	X	N	Q	w	E	x
X	X	x	l	l	X	x	x
t	Z	a	B	x	o	S	e
V	R	g	H	X	N	S	R
l	e	s	T	x	X	x	X

Find the Letter

Highlight the uppercase and
lowercase that start with the letter you are learning.

I Spy Letter

Highlight the uppercase and
lowercase that start with the letter you are learning.

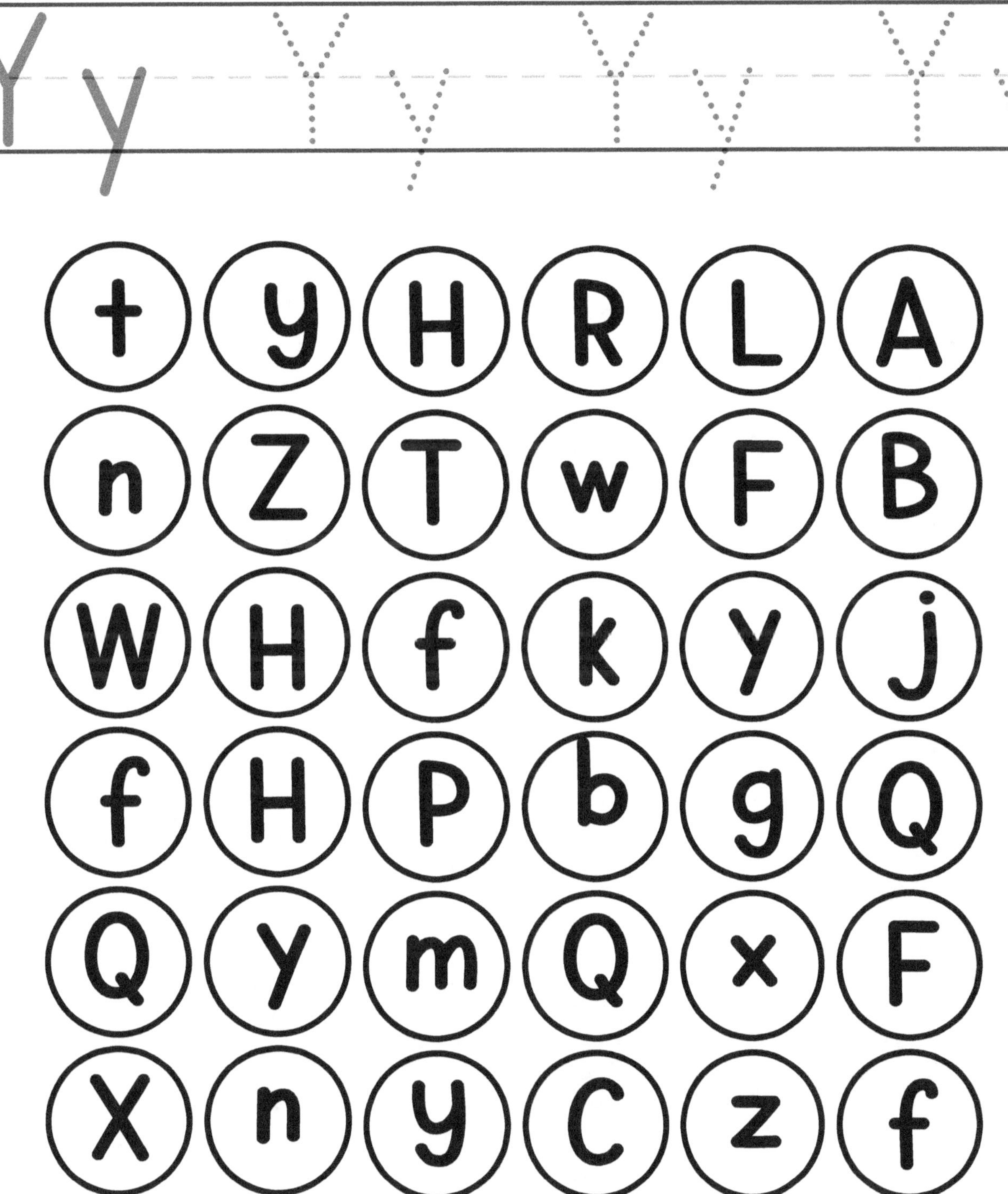

Letter Mazes

Highlight the uppercase and
lowercase that start with the letter you are learning.

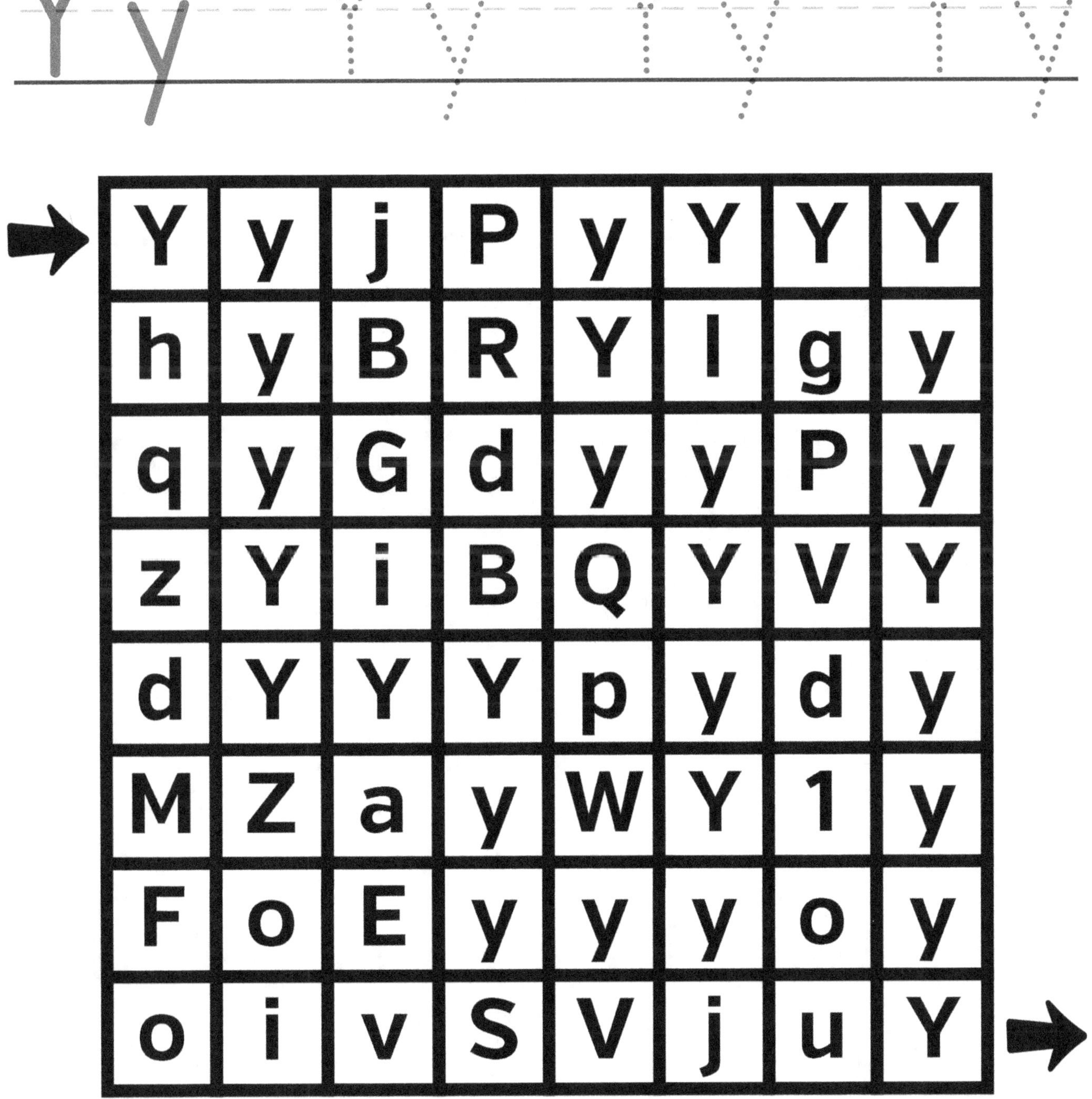

Find the Letter

Highlight the uppercase and
lowercase that start with the letter you are learning.

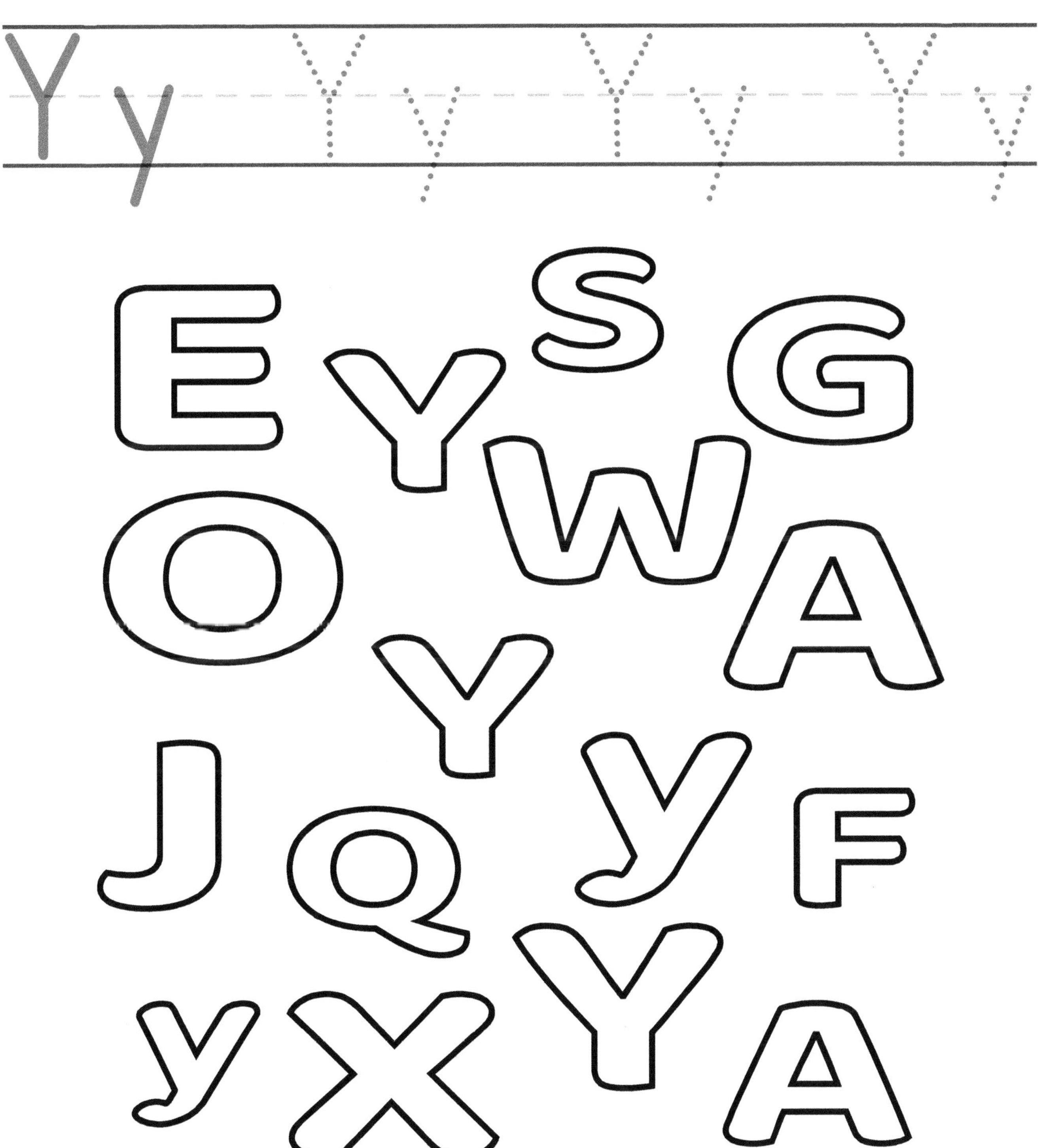

I Spy Letter

Highlight the uppercase and
lowercase that start with the letter you are learning.

Zz

t	y	H	R	L	A
n	Z	T	w	F	B
W	H	f	k	Y	j
f	H	P	b	g	Q
Q	Y	m	Q	x	F
X	n	Y	C	z	f

Letter Mazes

Highlight the uppercase and
lowercase that start with the letter you are learning.

Zz Zz Zz Zz

z	z	Z	u	Z	Z	z	z
w	l	Z	u	z	V	f	z
a	5	Z	O	z	t	p	z
u	H	z	z	p	p	Z	Z
B	l	i	l	m	B	z	l
V	r	o	C	Z	Z	z	i
E	o	E	W	z	N	S	p
F	h	d	s	z	z	Z	z

Find the Letter

Highlight the uppercase and
lowercase that start with the letter you are learning.

Z z

X S B G Y Z Z D J z W E z Z C C Z O